2/08

R. Smith

root awakenings

Vocabulary Development
Using Classical Word Roots

craig sirles
depaul university

STIPES PUBLISHING L. L. C.
CHAMPAIGN, ILLINOIS

Library of Congress Cataloging in Publication Data

Sirles, Craig
     Root Awakenings
     Vocabulary Development Using Classical Word Roots
     Includes Indices

Summary: Examines the formation of words from Latin and
            Greek roots

          1. English language – Foreign elements – Latin
          2. English language – Foreign elements – Greek
          3. English language – Roots 4. English language –
          word formation. 5. Vocabulary

ISBN 0-87563-581-4

Second corrected printing (2003)

Published by:

Stipes Publishing L.L.C.
204 W. University Ave.
Champaign, IL 61820

note to instructors

Root Awakenings: Vocabulary Development Through Classical Word Roots is an ideal basic text for courses devoted primarily to vocabulary enrichment and word history. It may also be used in first-year composition and rhetoric classes as well as in developmental college reading- and writing-skills courses. Because the pacing of material and test difficulty can readily be adjusted to different learning levels, *Root Awakenings* is highly suitable for accelerated college-preparatory classes at the secondary-school level. Even individuals planning to take standardized tests for admission to graduate and professional programs will find this text an invaluable study aid for the verbal sections of these tests.

There is no question of the need for textbooks covering word roots from Greek and Latin, the classical languages from which English derives the vast majority of its scholarly and technical vocabulary. The study of Greek dropped out of college curricula decades ago, and Latin has virtually vanished as a language studied in high schools and colleges. Yet when one considers that about 65% of all English words have their roots in Greek and Latin, and that a far higher percentage of newly-coined words derive at least partially from the classical languages, then one immediately appreciates how important a knowledge of classical word elements can be in helping to unlock meanings of words that confront students in their reading and listening, and that students are expected to use in formal writing and speaking.

Root Awakenings is not intended as a substitute for the study of any foreign language, but its systematic coverage of nearly 400 classical word elements, along with creative and stimulating exercises and questions that accompany these elements, will provide students and instructors alike with a formidable tool for greater vocabulary recognition. And an almost guaranteed bonus to users will be a heightened interest for the language they see and hear every day.

This text initially grew out of my experiences teaching a class in word etymology while I was still a graduate student. I loved the class, as did students, yet I found myself spending an inordinate amount of time devising lesson plans and test materials that were truly appropriate for an upper-level college course. Some years later I was charged with devising similar vocabulary-instruction material for faculty teaching developmental reading/critical thinking classes at DePaul University. These instructors had spent many years teaching college students, but few of them had had much experience teaching vocabulary.

My goal in writing *Root Awakenings* has been to create a vocabulary-building textbook for both students <u>and</u> instructors. The layout of the material is bright, not dense. Each lesson systematically clearly introduces a set of roots and meanings, plus copious examples of words formed from these root parts. The word-analysis and matching exercises are highly suitable for in-class drill and practice. Most of the discovery questions, which are designed to be mini-excursions into the dictionary, make ideal out-of-class assignments. Even the degree of difficulty of material can easily be adjusted to meet students' needs and course requirements: more advanced classes can cover lessons more quickly, and quizzes and other assignments can cover more lessons.

The first part of the text contains 20 Latin lessons, each covering 12 word roots (prefixes, stems, and occasionally suffixes) along with their variant spellings and meanings. The second part contains 10 Greek lessons, each with 15 root forms. We begin with Latin because, in general, its roots are far more useful in most language contexts: they form the bulk of educated vocabulary in English, irrespective of subject matter, and they are far more productive as vocabulary-building elements. Latin roots are also more problematic because of the many different spellings and meanings they can assume. In part, this explains why Latin lessons contain three fewer roots than do Greek lessons.

All Latin and Greek lessons follow the same format. Each "roots" page introduces students to a set of word parts in their various spellings, with the principal or most productive root spelling appearing first. Examples shown on the "roots" page give words containing all the spelling variants, though not necessarily all the different meanings, of the root. Students will also find the "notes" page useful for listing additional examples or other study information. The word-analysis exercises give students practice both in breaking down words into their constituent parts and in selecting the best root meaning among those available. The matching and definition exercises offer students more practice linking root parts to word meaning.

An important feature of *Root Awakenings* is the "discoveries" questions, which are intended to take students into areas beyond the lessons, introducing them to additional roots and words and sometimes to mysteries of word origins for which there may be no agreed-upon right answers. Each lesson concludes with an "awakenings" list of words containing newly introduced or previously covered roots; obviously, the prefixes, stems, and suffixes contained in each lesson appear in many more words than are listed on the "awakenings" pages. Comprehensive indexes of Latin and Greek roots and their meanings are located at the end of the text.

It is my hope that *Root Awakenings* sparks an enduring interest in words and language, both for you and for your students.   --Craig Sirles

contents

the study of word roots

A good vocabulary is one of the most valuable tools you can take into the classroom and into professional life. A rich voculary enhances reading comprehension and allows you to be a more effective communicator. Knowing the correct word--and knowing when to use it--not only makes you "sound" better in your essays and speeches; it also gives precision and clarity to what you have to say. Moreover, studies have shown that polished communicators are rated more capable, more intelligent, and even more reliable than less skilled writers and speakers. The aim of *Root Awakenings* is to increase your vocabulary and word-recognition skills through a study of word roots and their etymologies from the classical languages, Latin and Greek. To help you understand this better, we first need to answer a few questions.

Why Latin and Greek? Most of the common everyday words that we all learned as children are native or original words of the English language, but the more sophisticated words--those used in most formal situations or that we typically see in most books and newspapers--come principally from Latin and Greek. In fact, it is easy to list hundreds of nearly synonymous word pairs in English that contain one native word and another word containing elements from Latin or Greek: father-paternal, mother-maternal, heart-cardiology, water-hydraulic, light-illumination, thousand-kilometer. Indeed, the more one knows about classical languages, the more one knows about English vocabulary.

Why roots? It is actually a little inaccurate to suggest that "paternal," "maternal," or "cardiology" are Latin or Greek words; they clearly belong to the English lexicon, but they are made up of word parts (roots, prefixes, and suffixes) that derive from classical languages. "Photograph" comes from the Greek roots photo 'light' and graph 'write or record.' "Dentist" is made up of the Latin root dent, which means 'tooth,' plus -ist, a suffix meaning 'one who' that we find in such words as "violinist," "machinist," or "typist." Other words contain prefixes ("illegal" contains il- 'not,' the root leg 'law,' and the suffix -al, which indicates that the word is an adjective).

Why etymologies? And for that matter, what do we mean by the term "etymology"? Good dictionaries are more than guides to pronunciation, meaning, and usage of words. Under most entries in a college or unabridged dictionary, you will also find etymological information, which can include the original source language, root elements, and the earliest meaning of a word. Knowing the etymology of a word can deepen your understanding of the vocabulary you use everyday. For example, the word "senate" contains the Latin root sen 'old,' which we also find in "senior" and "senile." The etymology of "senate" gives us a clue about the earliest use of the word; in antiquity, the original Roman senate was a council of elders.

Etymological information is also useful in helping explain the meanings of words you don't know. All of us know what the word <u>confident</u> means. It derives from Latin <u>con</u>- 'very' or 'together' and <u>fid</u> 'faith,' and we can see how these two roots combine to produce the meaning of <u>confident</u>. Some of you might not be familiar with the word <u>diffident,</u> but if we know the meaning of the Latin prefix <u>dif</u>- 'not,' then we can see <u>diffident</u> means the opposite of <u>confident</u>. It is easy to see that the study of word etymology is an efficient way to build a richer vocabulary, to heighten your word-recognition skills, and, ultimately, to make you a better reader, writer, and speaker.

Knowledge of word roots alone will not improve your vocabulary. You have to carry many of the activities from *Root Awakenings* into your own reading. As you progress through the lessons, be consciously aware of the words you see and hear, especially those containing root parts you are currently learning. If you confront an unfamiliar word more than twice, always consult your dictionary. Look at the <u>entire</u> dictionary entry for defintion(s), pronunciation, and root makeup of the word. Remember that no one is born with a deep knowledge of words and meanings: we build a sophisticated vocabulary through constant, careful attention to what we read and hear.

using this book

Here are some pointers that will make your use of *Root Awakenings* more productive and efficient. While your instructor will be able to answer your questions about roots and word usage, there are still many unsolved mysteries surrounding the history and development of words in English.

In *Root Awakenings*, we define a prefix as a word part that can appear only at the beginning of a word, unless it is preceded by another prefix. Thus, intro-duce, introspective, and introversion all contain the prefix intro- 'within,' an element that normally occurs only in word-initial position. A number of English words contain two prefixes, however; reintroduce has both the prefix re-'again' and the prefix intro-. Most, though not all, prefixes in English carry prepositional (e.g. 'over,' 'under,' 'between,' 'across'), adverbial ('again,' 'badly,' 'not'), or intensifying ('very,' 'causing') meaning. In general, prefixes affect or alter the meaning of words in which they appear, but they almost never change the part of speech or supply other important grammatical information. Knowing what a prefix means gives you an important, but generally not an essential, clue about what a word means. Please note that all prefixes in *Root Awakenings* may be identified by a hyphen that follows the form (e.g., in-, post-).

Suffixes occur only at the ends of words unless they are followed by other suffixes. Dangerous, vigorous, and injurious all contain the adjectival suffix -ous, which itself can be followed by the adverbial suffix -ly (dangerously, vigorously, injuriously). Most suffixes in English provide grammatical infor-mation, such as part of speech (noun, adverb), but give little information about the meaning of the word. Suffixes play a very minor role in helping us recog-nize meaning of English words and, thus, receive only scant attention in the lessons. You will be able to identify suffixes in *Root Awakenings* by the hyphen that precedes the form (e.g., -fy, -ism).

Base roots may occur in any position in a word, and often we find more than one root in a single word. Roots form the nucleus of the study of word etymology because they reveal the original meaning and history of present-day words, and they provide the most important clues about word definitions. The great majority of word parts you will learn in *Root Awakenings* are base roots. Please note here that the word "root," as is suggested by the title of the textbook, is used both generically to denote all word parts and more narrowly to distinguish base root forms from prefixes and suffixes. These two usages of "root" should not confuse you, however, as the sentence context will make clear whether a generic or a narrow meaning is intended.

As you begin this program of vocabulary development, be aware of two areas of difficulty. One is that word parts frequently have more than one form; depending on adjacent letters and on where the root element appears in a word, a given word part may have numerous spellings. In most cases, the change in spelling is for ease of pronunciation of the word. For example, the form of the prefix in- 'not' varies predictably in the following words: incomplete, improper, irrelevant, illogical. As you study the word roots, you must learn all variant spellings. A greater difficulty you will encounter is that a given root may have multiple meanings. The prefix in-, along with all of its various spellings, means 'in' (influx), 'not' (impolite), 'cause' (endear), and 'very' (inflammable). When you run across a word containing the in- prefix, you must rely both on sentence sense and on common sense to determine which root meaning seems right. Very often several meanings may fit.

As you progress through the lessons in *Root Awakenings*, you will become aware of the cumulative nature of vocabulary development. With each new lesson, you will be combining word parts from earlier lessons with roots from later lessons, so you cannot simply forget roots on which you have already been tested: all roots, new and old, become current roots, all requiring regular review.

You will also find that a number of prefixes and root parts you learned in Latin lessons may appear with Greek word elements. The old rule for combining classical word elements, "Latin with Latin, Greek with Greek," works, for the most part; that is, the great bulk of English words derived from the classical languages contain either Latin or Greek elements, but not both; in fact, the only exceptions are recently coined terms, e.g., television (Greek tele- 'far' and Latin vis 'see'), sonogram (Latin son 'sound' and Greek gram 'write/record'). However, a number of Latin and Greek roots are identical or nearly so in spelling and meaning, e.g., gen 'kind/race' in Latin-derived generation and Greek-derived heterogeneous , or patr 'father' in Latin patricide and Greek patriarchy. In such cases, these roots are introduced only in the Latin lessons, and it is up to you to recognize them when they appear in the Greek lessons. The only way to ensure that you will remember them is by continually reviewing Latin roots as you are learning Greek forms.

Keeping most Latin and Greek forms straight in your mind is easier than may first appear. Greek-derived words are often scientific or technical terms with specialized concrete meanings. Latin-based words usually denote more general topics, and their meanings are often abstract or even metaphoric. For example, Greek pod 'foot' gives us podiatrist (foot doctor) and tripod (a three-footed support); the Latin equivalent ped produces not only pedal and pedestrian but also expedition, where the ped root suggests not just 'foot' but also 'movement.' This tendency toward abstract meaning can present a real challenge to mastering Latin forms, because root meanings often only suggest the definition of the word. Latin root elements produce many more English words, which is why the Latin is introduced first.

Lessons in *Root Awakenings* all follow the same format and order of presentation. Each Latin lesson consists of 12 word parts, while Greek lessons contain 15 root parts. You will also find all the variant forms and different meanings of each root item. The examples following each entry on this page are intended to illustrate the different forms of each word part but not necessarily all the different root meanings. For examples showing all of the meanings of a root element, refer to the "awakenings" list at the end of the lesson or consult your dictionary. Exercises and dictionary questions are intended to give you hands-on practice. Always do the exercises and questions, even if they are not assigned, because they will ultimately increase your knowledge of roots and allow you to see the parts "at work" with one another.

Rely on your instructor for tips on learning the roots in each lesson. Some instructors suggest that you prepare a flash card for each root; this method can greatly facilitate mastery of roots and meanings. Standard 3"-by-5" index cards make ideal flash cards. Write the various root spellings on one side of the card, indicating the lesson number and the number of different meanings carried by the root form. On the other side list each definition and provide one or two good examples of each different meaning. Choose examples whose root parts concretely reveal the meaning of the entire word. Pictured on the next page are the two sides of a sample flash card.

```
                                      Lesson 1


              con-, co-, col-,

                 con-, cor-


                                      2 meanings
```

(front side of flash card)

```
        together/with  =  COLLABORATION

                        =  COOPERATION


                  very  =  CONVIVIAL

                        =  CORRUPTION
```

(back side of flash card)

As your knowledge of these roots grows, so will your stack of flash cards. I suggest to my students that they keep cards for current roots together for quick and easy study, and that they alphabetize cards covering previously mastered roots for twice-a-week (or more frequent) review. The need to return to previously covered roots will become crucial once you start combining Greek and Latin. Remember: the first step in mastering classical roots, along with developing good skills for recognizing words containing these word parts, is memorization, yet the process of committing these roots to memory requires repeated exposure. There is no simply substitute for regular review of all the roots you have covered.

Your instructor will determine the content and frequency of quizzes, but in general you can expect to be tested on the word parts in some context. Many instructors will use questions that require you to break down words to their constituent parts and provide suitable meanings for each root part. Others will give multiple-choice or matching questions. In all cases, roots covered in earlier lessons will appear in each new quiz. Like learning a foreign language, you cannot conveniently forget what you covered in previous lessons.

Finally, you will need a good, up-to-date hardcover college dictionary to complete the assignments contained in this textbook. Many instructors specify which dictionary their students should use with *Root Awakenings*, but in the absence of a recommendation, make sure that the dictionary you select contains complete etymological information, including a full breakdown of the root parts making up each entry and a definition for each root part. Rely on your instructor for tips on dictionary use and on understanding etymological details contained in your dictionary.

It is impossible to overstate the importance of a good hardcover desk dictionary for use with this text. Do not skimp and buy a paperback version. Softcover dictionaries are good "take with" references, but they are no substitute for honest-to-goodness hardcover college dictionaries. No paperback dictionary on the market contains sufficient etymological information for you to answer many of the discovery questions in *Root Awakenings*. Moreover, a hardcover college dictionary is relatively inexpensive and will serve you throughout your academic and professional careers.

using your dictionary

Most people flip through the pages of dictionaries looking for spellings, definitions, or pronunciations. To students of words, however, a dictionary represents a great deal more: it is a vast treasure trove of information on correct or accepted usage, as well as on word history and etymology, part of speech, regional or specialized usages, and more. Because you can choose from among a half-dozen good college dictionaries on the market, and because dictionaries all differ slightly in the order and kinds of information they contain, you see here only a generic description of dictionary entries. Virtually all dictionary entries include these features:

entry word. This is the boldfaced head word or phrase for each separate entry. Individual words are divided into syllables by centered dots, while distinct words in phrases are not separated by dots. Thus, "stop sign" (appearing without a dot) is two separate words, but "stop•watch" (with a dot) is a single word. This system of syllable separation, known as syllabification, is useful in showing where we may split up and hyphenate single words at the ends of lines.

pronunciation. All dictionaries indicate word pronunciation by means of letters, letter combinations, phonetic symbols, and stress marks. The system for showing phonetic values differs from one dictionary to another, so you must learn with the system your dictionary uses. A key to pronunciation symbols and stress marks is found on every set of facing pages of dictionary listings. Many entries will have more than one pronunciation.

part of speech labels. Traditional parts of speech (noun, verb, adverb, etc.) are identified by lower-case italicized abbreviations (*n., v., adv.*). Verbs may be further described as transitive (*v. tr.* or *v. trans.*), meaning they can take a direct object, or as intransitive (*v. i.* or *v. int.*), if they cannot take an object. Many English words serve as more than one part of speech and are labeled as such in the entry.

inflected forms. Inflections are suffixes that show grammatical change in a word, such as verb tense. Dictionaries list all or most of the following: the four principal parts of verbs (past, progressive, and past participle); plural forms of nouns, especially if they are irregular or result in a spelling change; comparative and superlative degree forms of adjectives and adverbs.

definitions. Since so many words have multiple meanings, it is important to understand the ordering of definitions in a dictionary entry. Some dictionaries list the most commonly used meaning first, the second most common second, and so on. Others start with the most general meaning and then move to more specific usages. Still others begin with the oldest definition. Your dictionary's guide to usage will indicate the ordering used.

field labels. Meanings and usages that are specific to certain disciplines or areas of knowledge often receive italicized field labels, such as *music*, *chemistry*, *mathematics*, and the like.

status or usage labels. Status or usage labels us not only <u>what</u> words mean, but also <u>when</u> and <u>where</u> to use them. A common status label is "non-standard," which indicates a level of speaking or writing that educated people might consider incorrect. Other labels include "informal," "slang," "colloquial," "vulgar," "offensive," and "obscene." Consult the user's guide of your dictionary for explanations of these terms.

geographic and temporal labels. Dictionary entries frequently include geographic or temporal labels that associate a word or phrase with a particular geographic area or period of time. For example, geographic labels may indicate if a word or meaning typically occurs in British usage or in a particular dialect of America English. An "Archaic" label signals the word or meaning has dropped out of current usage.

etymologies. The word "etymology" derives from the Greek <u>etymon</u> and refers to the true or original meaning of a word. Etymological information, which always appears within square brackets, marks the path that words have taken as they moved from their earliest known sense and source language until they entered English. The word "etymology" is traceable back to Middle English and then to French, which took it from Latin, which borrowed it from Greek. Source languages and abbreviations contained in etymological listings are given in the user's guide of your dictionary.

extended forms. Dictionary entries can include words built from entry words. They often also list expressions and phrases containing entry words.

synonyms. Some dictionary entries list words with similar meanings. This is an especially useful feature if the word you are looking up is not the exact word you want to use.

For some practice using your dictionary, complete the following exercises:

1. What dictionary are you using? What is its date of publication?

    _____

2. Consult the introductory user's guide of your dictionary. What geographic, temporal, and usage or status labels are included (e.g., " British," "Southern U.S.," "obsolete," "slang," "informal," "disparaging," "vulgar," etc.)?

    _____

    _____

3. What phonetic symbols does your dictionary use for the following sounds?

    th in "then" _____   oo in "foot" _____   ss in "missile _____

    th in "thin" _____   oo in "fool" _____   ss in "fissure" _____

    th in "asthma" _____   oo in "flood" _____   sh in "fisher" _____

4. In slang usage, a "cretin" is an idiot. What is its surprising etymology?

    _____

5. What is an "assassin"? What is its etymology?

    _____

6. "Victuals" are supplies of food and other provisions. Record below your dictionary's pronunciation of this word. What do you find surprising?

    _____

7. Look up the meaning of "fortnight." What is its etymology?

    _____

practice exercises

Break the words listed below into their basic meaningful parts, separating prefixes and suffixes from the basic root forms. Identify the meaning of as many word parts (prefixes, roots, suffixes) as you can. In what way do the meanings of the parts give a clue about the meaning of the whole word itself?

1. semiannual _____

2. annuity _____

3. biannual _____

4. biennial _____

5. centennial _____

6. sesquicentennial _____

7. sesquipedalian _____

8. pedicure _____

9. curator _____

10. manicure _____

11. manacle _____

12. manuscript _____

13. nondescript _____

14. scriptorium _____

15. sanatorium _____

16. sanitary _____

Break each boldfaced word to its basic parts and give a suitable definition for each part. Refer to the root lists in Lessons 1 and 2 for root meanings. Do not define suffixes, but do consider what grammatical information these suffixes contribute to the word.

1. Adam **CONFIDED** in me about his secret plans to start his own company.

   _____

2. Successful writers all know that **REVISION** is part of the writing process.

   _____

3. Marianne always adds a humorous **POSTSCRIPT** to letters she sends me.

   _____

4. **CAPITALIZE** names of months (April, May) but not seasons (fall, winter).

   _____

5. Teenage **PREGNANCY** is a serious social problem in the United States.

   _____

6. Thom gives **DICTION** lessons to people planning careers in broadcasting.

   _____

7. Luxury automobiles are selling for **INCREDIBLY** high prices these days.

   _____

8. The **INSCRIPTION** on the gravestone had been worn smooth by weather.

   _____

9. Police **CONDUCT** an investigation whenever a person is reported missing.

   _____

10. It is a good idea to **VERIFY** the job history of any new employee you hire.

    _____

latin word roots

1   roots

Root Form	Root Meaning	Examples
1. **ben-, bon, bount**	good/well, generous	**ben**efit, **bon**us, **bount**iful
2. **cred, cre**	believe, trust	**cred**it, mis**cre**ant
3. **dict, dica**	speak, order, set forth/proclaim	**dict**ate, pre**dica**ment,
4. **fac, fect, fi(c), -fy**	make/do/deed	**fac**tory, in**fect**, magni**fic**ent, uni**fy**
5. **fid**	faith	**fid**elity
6. **gen(d), gener, gn, gon**[†]	race, kind, produce, birth/origin	**gen**der, **gener**ate, mali**gn**, **gon**ad
7. **in-, il-, im-, ir-, em-, en-**	in, not, cause, very	**in**come, **il**logical, **im**port, **ir**reverent, **em**power, **en**joy
8. **mal-**	bad/badly	**mal**icious
9. **post-**	after	**post**mortem
10. **pre-**	before	**pre**vious
11. **scrib, script**	write, record	**scrib**e, de**script**ion
12. **vit, viv**	life/live	**vit**al, con**viv**ial

[†]**gon** typically combines with Greek root parts (Lessons 21-30).

notes

exercises

WORD ANALYSIS: Break each boldfaced word down to its basic parts and give a suitable definition for each part. Ignore suffixes not covered in lessons.

1. Religious wars have been waged against peoples thought to be **INFIDELS**.

2. Senator McAllen resigned from office after being **INDICTED** for bribery.

3. I could not read the **INSCRIPTION** on the old tombstone in the cemetery.

4. The cut on Tobi's hand became badly **INFECTED**, causing her great pain.

5. Your own good deeds tend to **ENGENDER** good deeds from other people.

6. Mel was relieved that his tumor was **BENIGN** and did not require surgery.

7. The root parts of **PREPOSTEROUS** provide a good clue to its meaning.

8. Marchers in the Mardi Gras parade threw **BONBONS** to all the children.

9. The symphony held a **BENEFIT** concert to raise money for its new hall.

10. Teenage **PREGNANCY** is a matter of grave concern for school officials.

MATCHING: Match the correct definition to the words listed below.

_____ benison	A. weakness; disease; ailment
_____ bounteous	B. a short biographical account or record
_____ credence	C. capable of multiplying; giving offspring
_____ facility	D. active; full of energy; enthusiastic
_____ generative	E. order; command; directive
_____ malaise	F. charitable; lavish; plentiful
_____ postern	G. reliance; trust; faith
_____ prescription	H. blessing; prayer; grace; dedication
_____ vita	I. competence; skill; mastery
_____ vivacious	J. small rear gate or door to a castle or fort

BRIEFLY DEFINED: Give a short definition for the words listed below. Consult your dictionary for items you are unsure of.

posterior_____

infectious _____

malicious _____

diction _____

creed _____

discoveries

1. What is a bounty hunter? Connect the meaning of "bounty" to its etymology.

2. Distinguish a credible person and a creditable person.

3. The original meaning of "ditto," which comes from Italian, has changed considerably. Relate its present-day meaning to the dict root.

4. The legal term "affidavit" contains which root from this lesson? What is the meaning of this word?

5. Many people assist their communities through pro bono publico work. What is this?

6. Relate "ingenious" and "ingenuity" to "genius." How do these words differ in meaning? What is the meaning of the prefix in- in these words?

7. "Ingenuous" may be a word whose meaning you do not know. Look it up and distinguish it from "ingenious." What does "disingenuous" mean?

8. Consult your dictionary for the etymology of "malaria." What is its original meaning?

9. The following words all contain the root fac or one of its variant forms: confection, deficient, difficult, fact, factious, perfect, prefect. Consult the etymology of these words and then try to connect the meaning of the fac root with the overall meaning of the words.

10. The motto of the U.S. Marine Corps is "Semper Fidelis." What does this mean? How do confident and confidant(e) differ in meaning? What is a confidence game?

11. The word "credenza" is often used to denote a small office table or cabinet on which a typewriter or similar equipment may sit. Look up the etymology of this word. What was its original meaning?

12. Despite their appearances, "indicate," "indication," and "indicator" are not derived from the root parts in- and dica. Consult your dictionary for the etymology of these words.

awakenings

The following words are formed from word roots introduced in this lesson. Consult your dictionary for words you are unsure of. Use this list to awaken your word sense and help you master this lesson.

benediction	faculty	malaise
benefit	generation	malice
benign	generous	malign
bonbon	generic	posterior
bounty	genial	postscript
credentials	genital	predication
credenza	impregnate	prediction
credible	incredible	prefect
creditable	indict	pregnant
creed	infectious	preposterous
dictator	infidel	prescription
dictionary	ingenious	scribble
facet	ingenuous	Scriptures
facilitate	inscribe	vita
factor	malady	vitality

2   **roots**

Root Form	_Root Meaning_	_Examples_
1. **cap, capit, chap**	head, principal, property/money	**cap**e, **cap**ital, **chap**ter
2. **con-, co-, col-, com-, cor-**	together/with, very, cause	**con**temporary, **co**author, **col**late, **com**bine, **cor**rupt
3. **contr, counter**	against	**contr**aband, en**counter**
4. **dis-, di-, dif-**	not, apart/away, opposite	**dis**ease, **di**versity, **dif**ferent
5. **duc, duct**	lead	de**duc**e, con**duct**or
6. **ex-, e-, ef-**	out of, former	**ex**ception, **e**mit, **ef**fort
7. **man(u), main**	hand, do	**man**ual, **main**tain
8. **mand, mend**	order, require, praise	**mand**atory, recom**mend**
9. **ped**	foot, move, progress	**ped**al
10. **re-, red-**	again, back	**re**act, **red**undant
11. **ver**	true/truth	**ver**ily
12. **vid, vis, voy**	see	**vid**eo, super**vis**e, clair**voy**ant

notes

exercises

WORD ANALYSIS: Break each boldfaced word down to its basic parts and give a suitable definition for each part. Ignore suffixes not covered in lessons.

1. The President is the **COMMANDER** in Chief of the nation's armed forces.

2. Defense attorneys always try to **DISCREDIT** the prosecution's witnesses.

3. Jim never imagined that he would **ENCOUNTER** his son in New Mexico.

4. Ellis began a month-long **EXPEDITION** from Canada to the North Pole.

5. Paramedics **REVIVED** the small boy after he nearly drowned in the pool.

6. Harvey nearly lost his job for **CONTRADICTING** his new boss in public.

7. In the 19th century Britain was a world leader in **MANUFACTURING**.

8. **EDUCATION** involves more than teaching; it's also shaping young minds.

9. Lee overcame his speech **IMPEDIMENT** and became a successful actor.

10. Kitchen cleanliness helps prevent **INFECTION** from salmonella bacteria.

MATCHING: Match the correct definition to the words listed below.

_____ capitulum   A. festive; hearty; jolly

_____ chaplet   B. accurate; factual; authentic

_____ conduce   C. bind or restrain the wrists, as with prisoners

_____ convivial   D. summarize; relate or retell main points of a story

_____ envisage   E. conceive; imagine; consider

_____ expedient   F. dense cluster of small flower buds, as in broccoli

_____ manacle   G. promoting a purpose or interest; helpful; suitable

_____ mandamus   H. wreath of flowers worn on the head

_____ recapitulate   I. produce a specific result; contribute to an outcome

_____ veracious   J. directive given by a higher to a lower court of law

BRIEFLY DEFINED: Give a short definition for the words listed below. Consult your dictionary for items you are unsure of.

vista_____

pedestal _____

verity _____

duchy _____

mandate _____

discoveries

1. "Uninterested" means the opposite of "interested:" that is, an uninterested person has no interest in something. What is a "disinterested" person?

2. The dictator Benito Mussolini, who ruled Italy from 1922 to 1943, had the title "Il Duce." What do you think this phrase means? From what root does this title derive?

3. How does a confident person differ from a diffident person?

4. A "caprice" is a sudden impulse or change of mind, a "capricious" person is whimsical or fickle, and a "capriccio" is a musical work characterized by its free form. What is the strange etymology of these words?

5. Look up "counterfeit" in your dictionary. How do the root parts of the word contribute to its meaning?

6. We have the expression "pros and cons," which denotes reasons or people in favor of or opposed to some issue. The word "con" is a shortening of what prefix?

7. Occasionally a trial jury's "verdict" is perhaps not what the roots of the word suggest that it is. Explain.

8. "Efficient" and "efficacious" both contain the ef- (from ex-) and fic word parts. How do these words differ in meaning? Link the meaning of this prefix and root to the meanings of these words.

9. In this era of word processors, the term "manuscript" is probably etymologically inaccurate. Explain.

10. The term "pedigree" denotes a line of ancestors, particularly those involving purebred show dogs and thoroughbred race horses. Relate the curious etymology of this word to the idea of the family tree structure.

11. What is the difference between "capitulate" and "recapitulate"?

12. Relate the root duc/duct to the following words (some of which contain spelling forms of this root not included in this lesson): conduit, doge, ducat, duchess, duchy, duke, subdue.

awakenings

The following words are formed from word roots introduced in this lesson and in previous ones. Consult your dictionary for words you are unsure of. Use this list to awaken your word sense and help you master this lesson.

cap	encounter	manuscript
cape	difficult	pedestal
capitalism	disinfect	recapitalize
capitol	education	recapitulate
capitulate	efficiency	recommend
captain	evidence	reduce
caption	expedient	revise
command	expedition	revive
conducive	impediment	veracity
confection	induction	verity
confectionary	invisible	video
confidential	manage	visionary
conscription	mandate	visitation
contradict	manner	visor
contrary	manufacture	voyeur

3   **roots**

Root Form	_Root Meaning_	_Examples_
1. ad-, a-, ac-, af-, ag-, al-, am-, an-, ap-, ar-, as-, at-	to/toward, cause/make	**ad**hesive, **a**ver, **ac**climate, **af**fect, **ag**gravate, **al**lege, **am**munition, **an**nul, **ap**preciate, **ar**rive, **as**sembly, **at**tain
2. aud, audit	hear, listen	**aud**ible, **audit**ion
3. aur	ear, hear	mon**aur**al
4. cord	nice/agree, heart, remember	re**cord**
5. corp, corpor	body	**corp**uscle, **corpor**ation
6. de-	down, away, very	**de**mand
7. dent	tooth, hole/pit	**dent**ist
8. fer	carry, bear/birth	**fer**tile
9. son	sound	**son**ic
10. trans-, tra-	across/beyond, through	**trans**mit, **tra**verse
11. ven, vent	come	con**ven**e, **vent**ure
12. voc, vok	voice, call	**voc**al, pro**vok**e

notes

exercises

WORD ANALYSIS: Break each boldfaced word down to its basic parts and give a suitable definition for each part. Ignore suffixes not covered in lessons.

1. An old saying is "An ounce of **PREVENTION** is worth a pound of cure."

2. **ADVOCATES** of school reform demonstrated against cuts in the budget.

3. Jodie **INFERRED** from the sour tone of my voice that I was not satisfied.

4. Most desert regions are **INFERTILE**, making farming next to impossible.

5. Military units often suffered troop **DEFECTIONS** during the Civil War.

6. Many business organizations hold annual **CONVENTIONS** in Chicago.

7. Always remember to **INDENT** five spaces when you begin a paragraph.

8. Hal could not give police a detailed **DESCRIPTION** of the crime suspect.

9. The U.S. and Europe **DIFFER** on a number of important economic issues.

10. Our cat's **INAUDIBLE** cries failed to alert us that it was trapped upstairs.

MATCHING: Match the correct definition to the words listed below.

_____ advent   A. arrange a meeting or assembly of people

_____ affectation   B. declining in quality; failing; becoming inferior

_____ avocation   C. formal agreement or contract

_____ concordance   D. distraction or diversion, especially from work

_____ convoke   E. rich in tone; loud; echoing

_____ corpus   F. arrival; appearance; emergence

_____ covenant   G. yield or submit to the authority of another person

_____ defer   H. artificial display; unnatural or assumed behavior

_____ degenerative   I. a genetic trait or feature shared by twins

_____ resonant   J. a collection of writings on a specific subject

BRIEFLY DEFINED: Give a short definition for the words listed below. Consult your dictionary for items you are unsure of.

auriform_____

corpuscle _____

covenant_____

infer_____

sone_____

discoveries

1. Distinguish the verb "affect," the noun "affect," the verb "effect," and the noun "effect"? How does "affection" differ from "affectation"?

2. The following words all begin with the letter sequence v-e-n but are unrelated to the root ven meaning 'come': vending, venerable, venereal, venison, venom, ventilation, ventriloquist. What are the etymological makeups of these v-e-n words?

3. How do "supersonic" and "ultrasonic" differ in meaning?

4. According to its etymology, the phrase "out-of-tune accordion" is a contradiction in terms. Explain.

5. What is the difference between "demand" and "remand"?

6. What are the definitions of these words: sonant, sonata, sonatina, sonnet?

7. Distinguish "sonar" from "radar." Look up the etymology of these two words. Both these words are examples of acronyms. Explain what an acronym is. What other examples of acronyms can you think of?

8. Relate the root meaning of fer to the following words: confer, defer, infer, offer, prefer, refer, suffer, transfer. How do the different prefixes appearing in these words combine with the meaning of fer to produce the meanings of these words?

9. The meaning of "traduce" bears little relation to the root parts from which it derives. Consult your dictionary for the definition of this word.

10. The original meaning of the root dent was "tooth," but the root gradually assumed its second meaning, as in "dent" in a car fender. How do you think this second definition derived from the original root meaning?

11. What is the difference between "corporal" punishment and "capital" punishment? How do the etymologies help differentiate these two kinds of punishment?

12. Some word historians believe that the phrase "hocus-pocus" is related to the root corp. Check your dictionary for this possible connection.

awakenings

The following words are formed from word roots introduced in this lesson and in previous ones. Consult your dictionary for words you are unsure of. Use this list to awaken your word sense and help you master this lesson.

accordian	convocation	encircle
accredit	cordial	event
adventure	corporation	incorporation
advise	corpse	indentation
affect	corpuscle	invent
affectation	deceptive	preference
affidavit	deduction	refer
audit	defector	revenue
auditorium	defiance	sonata
aural	deficiency	sonic
concord	demand	sonnet
confer	dentures	sonorous
convenient	description	traduce
convent	difficult	transfer
covenant	disinfect	venture

4   **roots**

Root Form	_Root Meaning_	_Examples_
1. ante, anti	before, old	**ante**room, **anti**que
2. cap, capt, ceipt, ceiv, cept, cip, cup	take, contain, begin	**cap**acity, **capt**ure, re**ceipt**, con**ceiv**e, inter**cept**ion, re**cip**ient, oc**cup**y
3. circum, circ	around	**circum**flex, **circ**le
4. grand	great, full-grown	**grand**mother
5. loc, locat	place	**loc**omotion, **locat**e
6. locu, loqu	speak	**locu**tion, col**loqu**ial
7. magn, maj, max	large	**magn**ify, **maj**estic, **max**imal
8. sol	alone, comfort	**sol**o
9. sol	sun	**sol**arium
10. spec, spect, spic	look at, take note, appearance/form	**spec**ies, re**spect**, su**spic**ious
11. tang, tact, tag, tig, ting	touch, rely/depend	**tang**ent, con**tact**, con**tag**ion, con**tig**uous, con**ting**ency
12. vert, vers, vort	turn, highest point	per**vert**, **vers**atile, **vort**ex

     root awakenings

notes

exercises

WORD ANALYSIS: Break each boldfaced word down to its basic parts and give a suitable definition for each part. Ignore suffixes not covered in lessons.

1. Moscow and Rome are cities in Idaho and Georgia, **RESPECTIVELY**.

2. All students are required to attend the lecture tonight--no **EXCEPTIONS**.

3. The ship lost radio **CONTACT** with the U.S. Coast Guard before sinking.

4. American travelers are very **CONSPICUOUS** in Europe in the summer.

5. Telescopes **MAGNIFY** the stars and planets, making them visible to us.

6. A **TRAVERSE** curtain rod opens and closes draperies by means of a cord.

7. Consumer laws help protect us from **DECEPTIVE** business practices.

8. Controversy has surrounded the United Nations since its **INCEPTION**.

9. All people appearing on the quiz show received **CONSOLATION** prizes.

10. After three weeks alone in the Rockies, Bob experienced **DESOLATION**.

MATCHING: Match the correct definition to the words listed below.

_____ capacious   A. slightly related to or connected to

_____ collocation   B. center or focus of activity; point of concentration

_____ controvert   C. polished mirror used in optical instruments

_____ grandeur   D. back of a coin, medal, or page

_____ incipient   E. isolation or seclusion

_____ locus   F. developing; initial; opening

_____ solitude   G. arrangement of items in their proper order

_____ speculum   H. having lots of space or room

_____ tangential   I. brilliance; glory; stateliness

_____ verso   J. voice opposition to something; disapprove

BRIEFLY DEFINED: Give a short definition for the words listed below. Consult your dictionary for items you are unsure of.

adverse _____

averse _____

converse (noun) _____

converse (verb) _____

inverse _____

discoveries

1. A "grandfather clause" is a condition or provision in a law that extends special privileges to certain people or interests. Explain and exemplify.

2. In poker and similar card games, players must "ante up." What is the meaning of this term? Relate it to the root ante.

3. The cap root introduced in this lesson is found in the following words: anticipate, capable, exceptional, incapacitate, incipient, occupy, perceive, recuperate. Which of this root's three meanings best fits each word?

4. The United States is made up of 50 states, 48 of which are "contiguous." How does the root makeup of "contiguous" help define this word?

5. In 1215 the signing of the Magna Carta limited the power of English kings. What is the etymology of this historical document?

6. The verb "console" and the noun "console" have totally different meanings. Check your dictionary for the etymology of the noun "console."

7. Distinguish the following "verse" words: averse, adverse, converse, diverse, inverse, obverse, reverse, transverse, traverse.

8. Which of the following s-o-l words have the sol root meaning 'comfort'? which contain the 'alone' meaning? Which derive from the sol root meaning 'sun'?: solar, consolation, solitary, desolate, solace, solarium, soliloquy, solstice.

9. "Circus" comes from the circ root meaning 'round.' Look up its etymology and determine the connection between the root and its present meaning.

10. Look up the etymology of "expect," "expire," and "extant." What change occurs in the main root of these words when it combines with ex?

11. In 1863 President Abraham Lincoln signed the Emancipation Proclamation, thus officially ending slavery in the United States. How do the three root parts of "emancipation" reveal the meaning of this word?

12. Distinguish the following loc/locat words: local, locale, locality, locus, locomotion, locative, allocate, collocation, dislocation.

awakenings

The following words are formed from word roots introduced in this lesson and in previous ones. Consult your dictionary for words you are unsure of. Use this list to awaken your word sense and help you master this lesson.

accept	contraception	magnum
adversary	convert	majesty
antique	convertible	maximal
aspect	deception	reception
capacity	desolation	reverse
captivate	diversity	solar
captor	eloquent	solitary
circulate	except	specify
circumference	expect	spectator
circus	grandiose	tangible
colloquial	incontrovertible	versatile
console	insolate	version
conspicuous	intact	versus
contact	locus	vertical
contagious	locution	vortex

5   roots

<u>Root *Form*</u>	<u>Root *Meaning*</u>	<u>*Examples*</u>
1. amb(i), am	around, on both sides	**amb**iguous, **am**putate
2. anim	life/live, mind, soul/spirit	in**anim**ate
3. equ	fair, even/same, value	in**equ**ality
4. flect, flex	bend	re**flect**ion, **flex**ible
5. frag, fract, frang, fring	break, piece	**frag**ment, **fract**ion, **frang**ible, in**fring**e
6. mis, mit, miss, mess	send, allow	de**mis**e, per**mit**, **miss**ion, **mess**age
7. mis-	wrong	**mis**handle
8. par(t), peer, pair, port	equal/same, part, share	**par**ity, **peer**age, **pair**ed, pro**port**ion
9. par, para, pair	put in order, shield	pre**par**e, **para**sol, re**pair**
10. sequ, sec, secu, sue, suit	follow, series, ensemble, entreat,	**sequ**el, **sec**ond, con**secu**tive, en**sue**, pur**suit**
11. verg	bend, incline toward	con**verg**e
12. volv, volu	roll/turn, arise from	in**volv**e, re**volu**tion

notes

exercises

WORD ANALYSIS: Break each boldfaced word down to its basic parts and give a suitable definition for each part. Ignore suffixes not covered in lessons.

1. Alice's company imports men's **APPAREL** from Asia and South America.

2. Germany continues to pay **REPARATIONS** to victims of the Holocaust.

3. The furnace **EMITTED** a horrible odor that made the whole family sick.

4. An individual's **MISADVENTURES** can be comic, tragic, or even both.

5. "Be **PREPARED**" is the well-known motto of the Boy Scouts of America.

6. An **EQUIVOQUE** (voque = voc) is a pun or phrase having two meanings.

7. Thousands of visitors **CONVERGE** on New Orleans at Mardi Gras time.

8. Health officials will**COMMISSION** a study on children's dietary habits.

9. You are subject to a fine if you are convicted of a traffic **INFRACTION**.

10. Whenever George gets together with his brother, a big argument **ENSUES**.

MATCHING: Match the correct definition to the words listed below.

_____ ambit

_____ animism

_____ compeer

_____ diffraction

_____ flexor

_____ fractional

_____ missive

_____ par

_____ sequent

_____ voluble

A. change in the direction or intensity of radio waves

B. at a later time; arising from an earlier event

C. letter or written communication; correspondence

D. outside border or boundary; circuit

E. very small or insignificant; of little importance

F. philosophy that all earthly things possess a spirit

G. talkative; flowing with speech; fluent

H. muscle that controls movement in a joint or limb

I. one who is neither higher nor lower in rank

J. equality in value, number, or status

BRIEFLY DEFINED: Give a short definition for the words listed below. Consult your dictionary for items you are unsure of.

deflect _____

equation _____

flexible _____

remit _____

voluminous _____

discoveries

1. How do you think the meanings of the legal terms "sue" and "suit" are related to the <u>sequ</u> root meaning 'to follow'?

2. Not all words beginning with the e-q-u letter sequence derive from <u>equ</u> meaning 'fair/even/value.' From what Latin root do 'equestrian" and "equine" come?

3. What do following "animity" words mean: equanimity, longanimity, magnanimity, pusillanimity, unanimity?

4. Some telescopes magnify through a process known as "refraction." What does this term mean? What is the difference between "reflected" and "refracted" light?

5. How do "fragile," "frangible," and "fractious" differ in meaning?

6. The following words are made up of a prefix plus the root form <u>mit</u>: admit, demit, emit, omit, permit, pretermit, remit, submit, transmit. How do these different prefixes help produce the different meanings of these words?

7. From which <u>par</u> root does the word "disparage" come? What does this word mean?

8. In some churches worshipers genuflect when they pray? What does the root <u>genu</u> mean?

9. A "missal" is a prayer book used in the Roman Catholic Church. Despite its appearance, it is not derived from the <u>mit</u> root meaning 'send.' What is its etymology?

10. While most workers must maintain a regular schedule at their jobs, an increasing number of businesses offer "flextime." What is this?

11. The word "volume," meaning 'book,' derives from the <u>volu</u> root, which seemingly bears no connection to books. Account for this etymology.

12. Most individuals holding elective political office are people of high ambition. Interestingly, the original meaning of "ambition" was associated with political campaigning. Consult your dictionary for this connection.

awakenings

The following words are formed from word roots introduced in this lesson and in previous ones. Consult your dictionary for words you are unsure of. Use this list to awaken your word sense and help you master this lesson.

adequate	ensue	missile
admission	equality	missionary
ambition	equation	portion
animal	equator	pare
animosity	evolution	premises
apparatus	flexible	reflection
circumflex	fraction	refract
commission	fracture	remiss
committee	fragility	repair
consequential	inadmissable	sequel
converge	infraction	sequence
deflect	involvement	transmit
dismissive	misconduct	verge
diverge	misconception	volume
emission	misconduct	voluminous

6   roots

Root Form	_Root Meaning_	_Examples_
1. ab-, a-, abs-	away	**ab**normal, **a**vert, **abs**ent
2. ag, ig, act	do/act	**ag**ent, nav**ig**ate, re**act**ion
3. inter-, intel-	between/among	**inter**collegiate, **intel**ligence
4. intra-, intro-	within	**intra**state, **intro**duce
5. leg, legis, lect	law, charge/appoint, read, bequeath/grant	**leg**ality, **legis**late, **lect**ern
6. leg, lig, lect	choose/gather, esteem/care for	sacri**leg**ious, intel**lig**ent, e**lect**ion
7. ling, langu	language, tongue	**ling**o, **langu**age
8. liter	letter/writing	semi**liter**ate
9. parl, par, parol	discourse, promise	**parl**or, **par**able, **parol**e
10. tac, tic	silent	**tac**it, re**tic**ent
11. verb	word	pro**verb**
12. vol	wish/will	**vol**untary

notes

exercises

WORD ANALYSIS: Break each boldfaced word down to its basic parts and give a suitable definition for each part. Ignore suffixes not covered in lessons.

1. **INTROVERTS** are shy people who aren't very comfortable around others.

2. **INTERLINGUA** was developed for easier international communication.

3. The '*th*' in "thing" and "think" is classified as an **INTERDENTAL** sound.

4. A chemical **REAGENT** can detect or produce other chemical substances.

5. **ADVERBIAL** phrases gives sentences "when" and "where" information.

6. Adult **ILLITERACY** is a social problem in many Third World countries.

7. Children can now learn math using **INTERACTIVE** computer software.

8. The kidnappers **ABDUCTED** the diplomat and demanded a large ransom.

9. Danish is largely **INTELLIGIBLE** to speakers of Norwegian and Swedish.

10. The jury acquitted Higginson of **INVOLUNTARY** manslaughter charges.

MATCHING: Match the correct definition to the words listed below.

_____ actuate   A. very talkative; flowing with speech

_____ agenda   B. occurring in or performed on living organisms

_____ collected   C. having little to say; not very talkative

_____ intern   D. expressing a desire or intention; asking permission

_____ intravital   E. serious discussion; conference; debate

_____ languet   F. put into motion; launch; initiate; start

_____ parley   G. pointed and slender; shaped like a cylinder or rod

_____ taciturn   H. having self-control; unexcitable; calm

_____ verbose   I. arrest and confine, as prisoners of war

_____ volitive   J. schedule or program of things to be accomplished

BRIEFLY DEFINED: Give a short definition for the words listed below. Consult your dictionary for items you are unsure of.

lectern _____

legible _____

lingo _____

literal _____

verbiage _____

discoveries

1. Some people experience "vertigo" when they are high above the ground. What does this term mean? Relate its meaning to the <u>vert</u> and <u>ig</u> roots that make it up.

2. Many college students participate in "intramural" sports. How do these sports differ from "intercollegiate" athletic events? What is a "mural"? How does its meaning help define "intramural"?

3. Examine and explain the function of <u>ig</u> (and <u>eg</u>) in the following words: agitate, ambiguous, castigate, fumigate, fustigate, litigate, navigate, strategy, variegate.

4. Distinguish the following <u>leg</u> words: legacy, legatee, legator. Which of the meanings of this root is applicable for these words?

5. "Legumes," coming from an unrelated <u>leg</u> root, represent a family of vegetables. Which?

6. Look up the etymology of "sacrilege" and "sacrilegious." What does the root make up of these words suggest about their original meanings?

7. "Inter alia" is a Latin phrase akin to "etc." Distinguish these two terms.

8. "Linguine" is a type of pasta so named because its shape resembles little tongues. What is the meaning of these other varieties of pasta: fettucine, fusilli, penne, rigatoni, rotini, spaghetti, tortellini, vermicelli?

9. A "lapsus linguae" is a potentially embarrassing mistake that all of us make from time to time. What is its meaning and etymology?

10. Part of a medical doctor's training involves serving an "internship" at a hospital. What is this? Distinguish this word from a medical "externship."

11. During the nineteenth century many stately homes would have "parlors," which hosts would use for entertaining. Connect this word to the <u>parl</u> root. Another outdated term is "drawing room." What is its etymology?

12. What does it mean when a person give "tacit" approval for something. Is this type of approval implied or inferred?

awakenings

The following words are formed from word roots introduced in this lesson and in previous ones. Consult your dictionary for words you are unsure of. Use this list to awaken your word sense and help you master this lesson.

abduction	inactivity	illegibility
actionable	intellect	linguini
actuarial	intelligible	linguistics
adverb	intercept	literal
agenda	interim	parley
agitate	interlanguage	parliament
allegation	interlocutor	parlor
ambiguous	intermittent	parole
collect	internment	reagent
elect	intervene	reticent
elegant	intravital	tacit
enact	introduce	verbal
enactment	introvert	verbatim
illegality	legacy	verbify
illiterate	legend	volunteer

7   roots

Root Form	*Root Meaning*	*Examples*
1. ced, ceed, cess	move/go, withdraw, yield/let go	se**ced**e, suc**ceed**, re**cess**
2. cern, cert, cre, cret, crit	decide, separate	con**cern**, **cert**ain, de**cree**, dis**cret**ion, **crit**icize
3. cid, cad, cas, cis	cut, kill/die, fall, event/accident	sui**cid**e, **cas**cade, in**cis**ion
4. crim, crimin	judge, accuse, crime	**crim**e, **crimin**al
5. err	wrong, wander/go	**err**ant
6. jur, judic, judg, just	oath, right, judge	**jur**ist, **judic**ial, **judg**mental, **just**ice
7. pecc	sin, fault	im**pecc**able
8. pun, pen	punish, repent	**pun**itive, **pen**itent
9. scind, sciss	cut/split	re**scind**, **sciss**ors
10. sed, sid, sess	sit, stay/settle	**sed**iment, re**sid**ent, **sess**ion
11. seg, sec, sect	cut/split	**seg**ment, **sec**ant, inter**sect**ion
12. sert, ser	put forth, arrange	in**sert**, **ser**ies

    root awakenings

notes

exercises

WORD ANALYSIS: Break each boldfaced word down to its basic parts and give a suitable definition for each part. Ignore suffixes not covered in lessons.

1. You must establish legal **RESIDENCE** in a city or town in order to vote.

2. Television actors receive a **RESIDUAL** every time their show or ad airs.

3. The mayor **PRESIDES** over the city council and casts tie-breaking votes.

4. Mae's work is **IMPECCABLE**; her reports never contain miscalculations.

5. In earlier times people used magic spells to try to **CONJURE** up the dead.

6. Getting a refund was impossible until Jay **INTERCEDED** on my behalf.

7. **RECESSIVE** genetic traits don't necessarily pass to the next generation.

8. Samuel's visible **REPENTANCE** for the crime spared him a stay in jail.

9. Hal thinks he can park his car in handicapped spaces with **IMPUNITY**.

10. Nora **CERTIFIED** that the committee report was accurate and reliable.

MATCHING: Match the correct definition to the words listed below.

_____ adjure   A. release or surrender; to give up or give back

_____ ascertain   B. given to inactivity or lack of physical exercise

_____ cede   C. listed item by item; in exact order or sequence

_____ concision   D. cavity or indentation; hollow; nook or niche

_____ jurist   E. issue a command or order; direct or compel

_____ peccavi   F. stationary; permanently attached or fixed

_____ recess   G. to vouch for; to show to be true or authentic

_____ sedentary   H. expert or scholar of the law and the courts

_____ seriatim   I. formal confession of wrongdoing or guilt

_____ sessile   J. brevity; shortness in length or duration

BRIEFLY DEFINED: Give a short definition for the words listed below. Consult your dictionary for items you are unsure of.

decriminalize _____

dissertation _____

erroneous _____

peccadillo _____

residue _____

discoveries

1. What does it mean to act in "concert" with another person? What is a "concerted" effort?

2. "Concert" can also mean a musical performance. What do the following terms mean: concertina, concertino, concertize, concerto? What is the difference between a concerto and a symphony?

3. "Desert" is both a noun and a verb; as a noun, it has two distinctly different meanings. Consult your dictionary for the two noun definitions and the one verb definition of the word. Which form(s) of "desert" can be connected to the <u>sert</u> root introduced in this lesson?

4. Why are religious groups called "sects"? Connect the meaning of this word to its root makeup.

5. The <u>ced</u> root is found in a number of words: exceed, intercede, precede, proceed, recede. Why is "supersede" spelled with 's' and not with 'c'?

6. What is the difference between "discreet" and "discrete"? between "discern" and "concern"? between "certificate" and "certification"?

7. Publishers sometimes insert a loose sheet or page labeled "Errata" into a newly issued book. What does this word refer to?

8. What is the difference between "judicial" and "judicious"? between "jurisprudence" and "jurisdiction"? between a "jurist" and a "jury"?

9. The word "cascade" is etymologically redundant. Explain.

10. What is the difference between a "process" and a "procession"? between "proceedings" and "proceeds"? between "to proceed" and "to precede"?

11. <u>Cid</u> often means 'to kill,' as in "insecticide." What is the meaning of the following <u>cid</u> words: bacteriocidal, fungicidal, fratricide, genocide, homicide, patricide, regicide?

12. The Fifth Amendment of the U.S. Constitution guarantees protection from self-incrimination. What does the term "self-incrimination" mean? What do people often refuse to do when they "take the Fifth" in a court of law?

root awakenings

awakenings

The following words are formed from word roots introduced in this lesson and in previous ones. Consult your dictionary for words you are unsure of. Use this list to awaken your word sense and help you master this lesson.

access	dissertation	penalize
adjure	erratum	penance
assertive	erroneous	penitent
assess	excess	penitentiary
certify	incident	recession
certainty	incisors	reside
certificate	insert	residue
cessation	insidious	secant
circumcision	intersection	section
coincidence	judicial	sectarian
concede	judiciary	segment
concert	jurisdiction	sedan
concerto	juror	sedative
decisive	peccable	serial
desert	penal	series

roots

Root *Form*	*Root* *Meaning*	*Examples*
1. **ambl, ambul**	walk, move/go	**ambl**e, **ambul**ance
2. **cumber, cumbr**	hinder/hindrance	en**cumber**, **cumbr**ous
3. **cur, curr, curs, corr, cours**	run, hasty, path	in**cur**, **curr**iculum, **curs**ory, re**cours**e
4. **cur, sur**	care, attention	pedi**cur**e, in**sur**e
5. **extr, exter**	outside, beyond	**extr**avert, **exter**ior
6. **migr**	move/travel	im**migr**ation
7. **mov, mob, mot**	move, drive	**mov**e, **mob**, e**mot**e
8. **ob-, o-, oc-, of-, op-**	against, bad, not, very/to	**ob**ject, **o**mit, **oc**cult, **of**fend, **op**pose
9. **per-, pel-**	through, each, very, bad	**per**jure, **pel**lucid
10. **puls, pel, pell**	push/drive, beat	**puls**ate, pro**pel**, re**pell**ant
11. **sta, stan, stat, sti, stit, sist**	stand/stop, set up, be made up of	ob**sta**cle, in**stan**ce, **stat**ic, armi**sti**ce, de**stit**ute, re**sist**
12. **tort, tors, tor**	twist/turn, crooked	re**tort**, **tors**ion, **tor**que

notes

exercises

WORD ANALYSIS: Break each boldfaced word down to its basic parts and give a suitable definition for each part. Ignore suffixes not covered in lessons.

1. Despite its light weight, the dresser was very **CUMBERSOME** to move.

2. Doctors help those suffering from **INCURABLE** diseases live for years.

3. Sgt. Stiles was **DEMOTED** to the grade of private for disobeying orders.

4. During World War II the French **RESISTANCE** helped liberate France.

5. **OBSEQUIES** refer to the rites and ceremonies that honor a dead person.

6. Roberto is an **IMPULSIVE** shopper who buys whenever the urge strikes.

7. The number of Russian **EMIGRES** in the U.S. has dropped significantly.

8. Once a month Arlene will treat herself to a massage and a **MANICURE.**

9. Car **INSURANCE** is a funny thing: we buy it but hope we never need it.

10. There's always a lot of **COMMOTION** whenever the kids get together.

MATCHING: Match the correct definition to the words listed below.

_____ commove

_____ cumber

_____ currency

_____ curriculum vitae

_____ dispel

_____ incur

_____ peradventure

_____ perambulate

_____ restitute

_____ toroid

A. work résumé; record of one's accomplishments

B. eliminate; get rid of; make or be free of

C. doubt; chance; lack of certainty

D. bring back to an earlier condition; create anew

E. general acceptance, use, or custom

F. solid geometric object having a curved surface

G. clutter up; litter; get in the way

H. stroll through or around; meander; wander

I. accumulate; collect; gather; fall upon

J. agitate; stir; disturb; upset

BRIEFLY DEFINED: Give a short definition for the words listed below. Consult your dictionary for items you are unsure of.

amble _____

corridor _____

estate _____

impulse _____

torment _____

discoveries

1. How do you think the meanings of "career" and "curriculum" derive from the <u>cur</u> root?

2. What is the difference between printing and "cursive" writing? Link the etymology of this word to its meaning.

3. Some herbs are known for their curative powers. Explain what is meant by this.

4. Which direction or part of the word does the word "Occident" denote? Relate its etymology to the movement of the sun. What is the etymology of "Orient"? Contrast this word with "Occident."

5. What is the difference between an "official" and an "officious" person?

6. Account for the various meanings of <u>per</u> in the following words: percentile, perforate, permutation, perplexed, persecution, perspire, pervasive.

7. Account for the various meanings of <u>sta</u> and its related forms in the following words: assist, desist, exist, obstacle, obstinate, persist, stable, stage, standard, state, statue, statute, subsist.

8. What is the difference between "stationary" and "stationery"? Do you have a favorite mnemonic device that helps you differentiate these two words? (Refer to Lesson 29 for the root contained in "mnemonic.")

9. The summer and winter seasons begin with the "solstice." What is the etymology of this word? What do we call the days that begin spring and autumn?

10. Medical personnel typically transport victims of traffic accidents to the hospital in an "ambulance," but an injured party who is "ambulatory" might not need one. Explain.

11. The word "moment" derives from <u>mov</u> and is etymologically unrelated to "minute." Consult your dictionary for this connection to the <u>mov</u> root. What is the etymology of "minute"?

12. What is the difference between an emigrant and an immigrant? An emigre is a special kind of emigrant. Explain.

awakenings

The following words are formed from word roots introduced in this lesson and in previous ones. Consult your dictionary for words you are unsure of. Use this list to awaken your word sense and help you master this lesson.

accurate	emigrant	intercourse
amble	encumber	locomotion
ambulance	ensure	manicure
career	estate	mob
commotion	existence	motive
compel	exterior	movie
compulsory	extracurricular	obsequious
consistency	extradite	pedicure
constituency	extralegal	pervert
corridor	extremity	reinstate
curio	immigrant	remote
current	immovable	repulsive
destitute	incur	statue
disencumber	incurable	torsion
dispel	insure	tort

9   roots

Root Form	_Root Meaning_	_Examples_
1. doc, doctr	teach, accept	**doc**ent, **doctr**ine
2. grad, gred, gress	step/unit, go/move	**grad**e, ing**red**ient, pro**gress**
3. ject, jac, jet	throw, send, situated	in**ject**, ad**jac**ent, **jet**
4. pon, pos, post, pound	place/put	op**pon**ent, **pos**ition, com**post**, im**pound**
5. port, por	carry, opening, gate	ex**port**, **por**ous
6. pro-	before, forward, instead of, for/on behalf of	**pro**mote
7. retro-	backward, earlier	**retro**fit
8. se-	apart	**se**cession
9. solu, solv	loosen, answer	re**solu**tion, **solv**ent
10. sub-, suc-, suf-, sup-, sur-, sus-	under, less than, after, small/minor	**sub**par, **suc**ceed, **suf**fer, **sup**port, **sur**rogate, **sus**pend
11. super-, sur-, supr-, sum(m)	over, more than, large/major, total, highest	**super**vise, **sur**vive, **supra**national, **summ**ary
12. ultra-, ult	final, beyond, other	**ultra**sonic, **ult**imate

notes

exercises

WORD ANALYSIS: Break each boldfaced word down to its basic parts and give a suitable definition for each part. Ignore suffixes not covered in lessons.

1. Quinton should stop **INJECTING** his opinions into our conversations.

2. The tyrannical dictator was **DEPOSED** by members of the armed forces.

3. The pay raise for union members was made **RETROACTIVE** to July 1st.

4. In criminal trials **PROSECUTORS** always present their witnesses first.

5. Ailene looked calm and **COMPOSED** as she addressed the senior class.

6. Mark's house is **ADJACENT** to the grocery store, making shopping easy.

7. The rules of football allow coaches to **SUBSTITUTE** players frequently.

8. Some people are convinced that prayer **ABSOLVES** them from their sins.

9. Some workers need lots of **SUPERVISION** while others need none at all.

10. Automatic teller machines allow you to make **DEPOSITS** electronically.

MATCHING: Match the correct definition to the words listed below.

_____ abject	A.	attitude; frame of mind; assumed mental stance
_____ appositive	B.	driving or thrusting forward; impelling
_____ disport	C.	extremism; radicalism; excessive severity
_____ doctrinaire	D.	amuse oneself through distraction
_____ gradation	E.	side-by-side; located next to one another
_____ jactitation	F.	lowly; wretched; totally worthless; miserable
_____ posture	G.	decay; decline; worsen; deteriorate
_____ projectile	H.	change in successive stages, tones, or shades
_____ regress	I.	stubbornly inflexible; clinging to a single belief
_____ ultraism	J.	extreme restlessness in bed; tossing and turning

BRIEFLY DEFINED: Give a short definition for the words listed below. Consult your dictionary for items you are unsure of.

composition _____

doctrine _____

exponent _____

objective _____

submission _____

discoveries

1. Police artists often draw "composite" pictures that aid witnesses in the identification of crime suspects. Why are such drawings given this name?

2. Distinguish the following pos words: appose, compose, depose, expose, impose, oppose, prepose, propose, repose, suppose, superpose, transpose.

3. If you visit a museum, you might encounter a "docent." What is this person's function? Where else might you find "docents"?

4. It has been said that the circus magnate P. T. Barnum would cheat unsuspecting customers by charging them admission fees and luring them into an exhibition or show that displayed the following sign, "To the Egress." Explain Barnum's purported deception.

5. Which of the various meanings of the prefix pro- do you find in the following words: profess, proficient, prolong, promiscuous, promote, propose, proscription, prospect, proverb?

6. What is the difference between "progeny" and "progenitor"?

7. Distinguish "importation," "importance," and "importunity." In what way does "opportunity" have a largely positive meaning while "opportunistic" is negative?

8. Look up the etymology of "sport." What was its original meaning?

9. Differentiate the following "ject" words: abject, conjecture, dejected, eject, injection, projection, reject, trajectory. How does the ject root help shape the meanings of these words?

10. The phrase "flotsam and jetsam" was originally a nautical term. How is this expression generally used today? What are the etymologies of "flotsam" and "jetsam"?

11. What are you doing when you give someone an "ultimatum"? Should you trust someone who has an "ulterior" motive? Explain.

12. Look up the etymology of "document." What was the earliest meaning of this word? How is its first meaning connected to the root doc?

awakenings

The following words are formed from word roots introduced in this lesson and in previous ones. Consult your dictionary for words you are unsure of. Use this list to awaken your word sense and help you master this lesson.

absolve	objective	retroflex
adjacent	opportunity	seduction
compose	port	select
dejected	porter	subscribe
disport	portico	substitute
docent	pose	superstitious
doctor	position	supervise
doctrine	positive	support
document	preposition	suppose
egress	procedure	survive
export	process	suspect
gradual	promise	transport
important	prosecute	ulterior
inject	report	ultimatum
jetsam	retroactive	ultra

10   roots

<u>*Root* Form</u>	<u>*Root* Meaning</u>	<u>*Examples*</u>
1. **am(a), amor, em, (i)m**	love, friendly	**ama**teur, **amor**ous, en**em**y, in**im**ical
2. **fam(il)**	household, know	**famil**iarize
3. **feder**	league/union	**feder**alism
4. **fil(i)**	child/offspring, related	af**fili**ation
5. **frat(e)r**	brother, allied	**fratr**icide
6. **hom, homin, hum(b)**	human, earth, low	**hom**o sapiens, **homin**id, **humb**le
7. **mat(e)r, metr**[†]	mother, womb/origin, substance	alma **mater**, **metr**opolitan
8. **nat, gnat, nasc, gnit**	source, born, tribe	**nat**ive, co**gnat**e, **nasc**ent, co**gnit**ive
9. **pat(e)r**	father, support, homeland	**pater**nity
10. **prol**	offspring	**prol**ific
11. **sangui**	blood, red, optimistic	**sangui**nary
12. **vir, virtu**	man, true/real, skill	**vir**ile, **virtu**oso

[†]**metr**, which is etymologically related to **mat(e)r**, typically combines with Greek roots (Lessons 21-30).

notes

exercises

WORD ANALYSIS: Break each boldfaced word down to its basic parts and give a suitable definition for each part. Ignore suffixes not covered in lessons.

1. The Marines encountered heavy **ENEMY** fire as soon as they hit the beach.

2. Mothers-to-be should receive **PRENATAL** care early in their pregnancies.

3. The **CONFEDERACY** was made up of 11 slave-holding Southern states.

4. According to the Bible, Abel was the first to fall victim to **FRATRICIDE**.

5. Many medical schools are **AFFILIATED** with major research hospitals.

6. Mindy is not at all **ENAMORED** of Dennis; in fact, she can't stand him.

7. Legally speaking, **COMPATRIOTS** hold passports from the same nation.

8. We've seen a **RENASCENCE** in civic pride since the mayor took office.

9. Many young people are disturbed by **INHUMANE** treatment of animals.

10. Veterans groups work hard to locate and **REPATRIATE** prisoners of war.

MATCHING: Match the correct definition to the words listed below.

_____ amatory	A.	send or return to one's place of birth or origin
_____ enate	B.	mingle, associate, or keep company with others
_____ federalism	C.	murderous; involving carnage or bloodshed
_____ fraternize	D.	beginning; coming into existence
_____ homunculus	E.	related maternally; stemming from the mother
_____ nascent	F.	particular knowledge or expertise in the fine arts
_____ prolific	G.	form of government using centralized authority
_____ repatriate	H.	very small person; undersized individual; pygmy
_____ sanguineous	I.	sexually provocative; given to lust
_____ virtu	J.	producing or generating great works or results

BRIEFLY DEFINED: Give a short definition for the words listed below. Consult your dictionary for items you are unsure of.

affiliation _____

alma mater _____

federation _____

Renaissance _____

virtuoso _____

discoveries

1. What does the etymology of "amateur" reveal about the original meaning of this word? What various meanings does the word have today?

2. What is the difference between "amiable" and "amicable"? Which of these words are you more likely to find in legal contexts?

3. Compare <u>homo</u> in "homo sapiens" with the <u>homo</u> root found in "homogeneous," "homogenize," "homonym," and "homosexual." What is the difference in these two roots?

4. Distinguish the words "material" and "materiel." Define the legal terms "material witness" and "material evidence." What do we mean when we call a person "materialistic"?

5. Look up the following <u>patr</u>-derived words in your dictionary: patroclinous, patrilocal, patrimony, patristic, patronage, paternalism. Which one of this root's various meanings best applies to each of these words?

6. Connect "friar" to a root in this lesson? What does this word mean? What courtesy title (Mr., Ms., etc.) would be accorded a friar?

7. The fruity Spanish wine "sangria" and the French expression "sang-froid" both derive from the <u>sangui</u> root. Explain their connection.

8. "Proletariat" denotes members of the working class and is distinguished from the "bourgeoisie," which is the middle class. Try to connect the root meaning of <u>prol</u> to "proletariat." What is the etymology of "bourgeoisie"? What do these terms mean in Marxist economic theory?

9. What is the difference between "patrilineal" and "matrilineal" societies?

10. "Patronize" has two very distinct meanings, one positive and one negative. What are they?

11. What is the meaning of the following "family" phrases: family tree, family circle (in a theater), family style (in a restaurant), family planning?

12. Not all v-i-r words derive from the <u>vir</u> root meaning 'man, true/real, skill.' Locate words in your dictionary that come from two other <u>vir</u> roots.

awakenings

The following words are formed from word roots introduced in this lesson and in previous ones. Consult your dictionary for words you are unsure of. Use this list to awaken your word sense and help you master this lesson.

affiliation	fraternize	native
amateur	fratricide	nativity
amicable	homage	nature
amorous	homicide	paternal
cognate	hominid	patriotic
confederate	homo sapiens	patriotism
enate	humane	patronize
enemy	humble	prenatal
exhume	material	proletarian
familiarize	materiel	proletariate
family	maternal	repatriate
federal	maternity	sanguinolent
federated	matrimony	unfamiliar
federation	matrix	virtual
filly	matronly	virtue

11   **roots**

Root Form	_Root Meaning_	_Examples_
1. **cult, col**	dwell, till, worship	**cult**ivate, **col**ony
2. **div, de(i)**	god, foretell	**div**inty, **dei**ty
3. **dom, domin**	house, control, master/lord	**dom**ain, **domin**ion
4. **greg**	flock/group	con**greg**ation
5. **multi**	many	**multi**national
6. **omni**	all	**omni**directional
7. **plic, plex, pli, pl, -ply**	layer, fold, tangle	ap**plic**ation, com**plex**, **pli**able, tri**pl**e, re**ply**
8. **pot, poss**	power, able	**pot**ent, **poss**ible
9. **reg, rig, rect**	rule/ruler, right, straight	**reg**ent, incor**rig**ible, e**rect**
10. **sac(e)r, secr, sanct**	sacred, secret	**sacr**ament, con**secr**ation, **sanct**uary
11. **soci**	group, ally, companion	as**soci**ation
12. **vulg**	common, low	**vulg**arity

notes

exercises

WORD ANALYSIS: Break each boldfaced word down to its basic parts and give a suitable definition for each part. Ignore suffixes not covered in lessons.

1. The suppliers promised to **RECTIFY** the billing error and issue us a credit.

2. India's extreme **MULTILINGUALISM** presents challenges to educators.

3. Most Canadians speak English, but French **PREDOMINATES** in Quebec.

4. The **CONGREGATION** quietly filed out of church following the funeral.

5. The police suspected Arthur of serving as an **ACCOMPLICE** to the crime.

6. A half century ago we thought of travel in space as an **IMPOSSIBILITY**.

7. The Department of **CORRECTIONS** hopes to rehabilitate prison inmates.

8. Jonathan attended a seminar given by one of his business **ASSOCIATES**.

9. Memorial Day honors those soldiers who made the supreme **SACRIFICE**.

10. Manufacturers should be in **COMPLIANCE** with state air pollution laws.

MATCHING: Match the correct definition to the words listed below.

_____ deify   A. having numerous small compartments or cavities

_____ dissociation   B. coarse; having no manners or refinement

_____ dominical   C. in Christianity, associated with Jesus Christ

_____ explicate   D. capable of increasing; expanding; reproducing

_____ incult   E. worship; adore; hold in high esteem;

_____ multilocular   F. very private place; room that may not be violated

_____ multiplicative   G. phrase used only in speech; nonstandard word

_____ potentate   H. in psychology, development of many personalities

_____ sanctum sanctorum I. make understandable; clarify the meaning of

_____ vulgarism   J. monarch or ruler; person having total command

BRIEFLY DEFINED: Give a short definition for the words listed below. Consult your dictionary for items you are unsure of.

domestication _____

multitude _____

potentiality _____

regime _____

sociable _____

discoveries

1. A "major-domo" is the person in charge of a large estate or mansion. How does its etymology reveal the meaning of this word?

2. Horses and oxen are examples of "domesticated" animals. What does this word mean? Which of the following animal species are also domesticated: cats, pigs, gold fish (in an aquarium), minks, goats, eagles, buffalo? Find other examples of domesticated and undomesticated creatures.

3. A page in a book labeled "Corrigenda" refers to what? Compare this word with "Errata," which was covered in an earlier lesson.

4. "Region," "realm," and "real estate" are all etymologically related to the reg root. How would you explain the connection between this root and words denoting property or territory?

5. Look up the meaning of "deism." What are the religious and philosophical beliefs of deists?

6. Occasionally in motion pictures and television shows set in the American West, we see people using "divining rods." What is their alleged purpose?

7. What is the difference between "explicit" and "implicit"? between "explain" and "explicate"? between "imply" and "implicate"? between "complicity" and "complicate"?

8. The "dirigible" is a lighter-than-air craft that was eventually replaced by the airplane as a means of long-distance air travel. What do its root parts mean? What is the more common name for the dirigible?

9. What do we mean when we call someone a "sacrificial lamb"? What is a "sacred cow"? What is a "sacrifice fly" in baseball? What state capital contains the sacr root in its name?

10. What is "vulgar Latin"?

11. What do the following "culture" words mean: agriculture, aquiculture, arboriculture, horticulture, pisciculture, viniculture?

12. What is "socialism"? Compare and contrast socialism and communism.

awakenings

The following words are formed from word roots introduced in this lesson and in previous ones. Consult your dictionary for words you are unsure of. Use this list to awaken your word sense and help you master this lesson.

accomplice	dirigible	potent
aggregate	divinity	predominant
applicant	domain	regal
apply	domineer	regimen
association	gregarious	regulate
colonize	implication	reply
colony	impotent	sacrament
complication	incorrigible	sacred
congregation	multicultural	sanctimonious
correct	multilingual	sanction
cultivate	multiplication	sanctuary
cultural	multiplicity	social
deist	multiply	socialism
deity	pliers	sociocultural
directional	possible	vulgate

12   roots

Root Form	*Root Meaning*	*Examples*
1. aug, augur, auct, aux	increase, divine, help	**aug**ment, **augur**y, **auct**ion, **aux**iliary
2. cresc, creas, cre, cru	grow/growth	**cresc**ent, in**creas**e, in**cre**ment, ac**cru**e
3. cruc, cru	cross, torment important test	**cruc**ify, **cru**x
4. fa, fam, fess	speak, spoken of, rumor	**fa**ble, in**fam**y, pro**fess**or
5. fig, fict, fing, fix, -fy	shape/make, invent, fasten	**fig**urine, **fict**ious, **fing**er, **fix**, cruci**fy**
6. gest, ger	carry, offer, clog	in**gest**, belli**ger**ent
7. linqu, lic	leave/forsake, permit	re**linqu**ish, re**lic**
8. ora, or	formal speech, pray	**ora**tory, ad**ore**
9. quest, quer, quir, quis	ask, seek, catch	con**quest**, **quer**y, re**quir**e, in**quis**itive
10. quie, quit, quil	quiet, rest	**quie**t, **quit**, tran**quil**
11. robor, robus	strength	cor**robor**ate, **robus**t
12. roga	ask, propose, take away	inter**roga**tive

notes

exercises

WORD ANALYSIS: Break each boldfaced word down to its basic parts and give a suitable definition for each part. Ignore suffixes not covered in lessons.

1. At Catholic schools you'll often find **CRUCIFIXES** in every classroom.

2. Romy was subjected to harsh **INTERROGATION** by police detectives.

3. The Presidential **INAUGURATION** is both a solemn and a festive event.

4. Uncle Charlie has a **DISFIGURING** facial scar from his wartime wound.

5. Juvenile **DELINQUENCY** is on the rise despite job programs for youth.

6. Some people may find sleep aids and **TRANQUILIZERS** habit-forming.

7. Dr. Issacson recommended a **DECONGESTANT** for my stuffed-up nose.

8. Garrison is planning to sue the newspaper for character **DEFAMATION**.

9. The coroner will conduct an **INQUEST** into the drowning victim's death.

10. With some charge accounts interest **ACCRUES** from the date of purchase.

MATCHING: Match the correct definition to the words listed below.

_____ accrete	A. one overlapping the other, as insect wings at rest
_____ augmentative	B. thorough study of a subject, as a master's thesis
_____ confabulate	C. making more robust; adding strength or quantity
_____ cruciate	D. swelling or outgrowth, such as a wart or cyst
_____ disquisition	E. order or revelation from God; sacred prediction
_____ excrescense	F. chat; converse with someone informally
_____ fabulist	G. ignoring accepted rules of behavior; immoral
_____ gestation	H. make larger or more numerous; multiply
_____ licentious	I. liar; inventor of stories; teller of falsehoods
_____ oracle	J. conception and full development of a plan or idea

BRIEFLY DEFINED: Give a short definition for the words listed below. Consult your dictionary for items you are unsure of.

arrogance _____

derelict _____

figurine _____

infamy _____ _____

query _____

discoveries

1. The word "cereal" is related both to the name of a Roman goddess and to a root contained in this lesson. Identify the goddess and the root. Try to account for the semantic connection between "cereal" and this root?

2. It is said that many hearts have been broken by "unrequited" love. What is this? What root parts make up this word?

3. Define the word "fixation"? What is the meaning of "fixative"? What is an "idée fixe"? What is a "prix fixe" dinner? Consult your dictionary for the pronunciation of these last two phrases, both coming from French.

4. What does "gestate" mean? Approximately how long do the following species gestate: cows, elephants, horses, humans, monkeys, pigs, rabbits? Do birds gestate? Why or why not?

5. "Auction" comes from the <u>aug</u> root. What does this word mean? What is the connection between the word and the root?

6. "Crescendo" and "decrescendo" are musical terms? What do they mean? Link their root parts to their definitions.

7. Many people "gesticulate" when they speak. Define this word. What is its etymology?

8. "Inquisitive" means 'curious' or 'eager to learn or gain knowledge.' The related term "inquisition" oftentimes carries a negative meaning. Explain. What historical event is denoted by "the Inquisition"?

9. The gravestone inscription "R.I.P." is often thought to stand for the English phrase "rest in peace," but it is actually a Latin abbreviation. What is this Latin phrase? What root from this lesson is contained in "R.I.P."?

10. Distinguish "corroborate," "collaborate," and "cooperate."

11. Consult your dictionary for the curious etymologies of "infant" and "infantry." What does the French phrase "enfant terrible" mean?

12. The English lexicon expands greatly through the use of "affixes." What are they? What types of affixes exist in English? Exemplify.

awakenings

The following words are formed from word roots introduced in this lesson and in previous ones. Consult your dictionary for words you are unsure of. Use this list to awaken your word sense and help you master this lesson.

accrue	delinquent	ingest
acquire	disquiet	interrogative
acquittal	effigy	license
adore	excruciating	orate
affix	fabulous	preface
arrogance	fiction	profess
auction	figurine	professional
concrete	finger	quest
confession	gerund	quit
congest	gesture	quite
corroboration	inaugural	recruit
crucial	increase	requirement
Crusades	infant	suffix
crux	inquire	suggest
defame	indigestion	tranquilizer

13 roots

Root Form	Root Meaning	Examples
1. fin	end, border, pay/pay off	confine
2. hes, her	stick/cling	adhesive, coherent
3. jun(c)t, join, jug	connect/join, impose	juncture, enjoin, jugular
4. limit, limin	threshold	limited, subliminal
5. mem(or)	recall	remember
6. ment, mon(t), min, men, mount	think, advise, warn/threaten, serve, project/mountain, lead	mental, monitor, minister, menial, mountaineer
7. ratio, rat	reason, calculate	irrational, rate
8. sent, sens	feel, message, opinion	sentence, sensible
9. tempt, tent	attract, try, touch	temptation, tentative
10. ten, tin, tent, tain	hold, keep	tenant, continual, intention, retain
11. tend, tens, tent, tenu	stretch, lean toward, heed, thin/delicate	extend, tense, attentive, tenuous
12. tract, tra, trai, treat	draw/drag, treat/care	retract, portray, trailer, treaty

notes

exercises

WORD ANALYSIS: Break each boldfaced word down to its basic parts and give a suitable definition for each part. Ignore suffixes not covered in lessons.

1. Amanda may live with her parents as long as she **ADHERES** to their rules.

2. Josh is a very confused man who has ill-**DEFINED** plans about his future.

3. After much heated debate Congress finally **RATIFIED** the peace treaty.

4. Attorneys receive **RETAINER** fees for services they provide their clients.

5. The invading army destroyed the city and **SUBJUGATED** its inhabitants.

6. At annual homecoming festivities alumni get together and **REMINISCE**.

7. Kyle became **IRRATIONAL** when his girlfriend left him for another guy.

8. "And," "or," "yet," "but", and "so" are coordinating **CONJUNCTIONS**.

9. The committee held a **PRELIMINARY** meeting to plan sales strategies.

10. Natural resources are not **INFINITE**; therefore, we must conserve them.

MATCHING: Match the correct definition to the words listed below.

_____ ament   A. architectural ornament found atop an archway

_____ appertain   B. small secret group united by common interests

_____ conjugal   C. person having a low or undeveloped intellect

_____ detent   D. answer or reply sharply to a statement

_____ finial   E. pertaining to marriage or married partners

_____ junta   F. logical and methodical; carefully considered

_____ presentiment   G. knowledge of the future; belief in a future event

_____ ratiocinative H. aware; conscious; having knowledge of

_____ rejoin   I. belong to; have a role or function in

_____ sentient   J. mechanical catch or lever that locks a mechanism

BRIEFLY DEFINED: Give a short definition for the words listed below. Consult your dictionary for items you are unsure of.

memoirs _____

ratio _____

sentinel _____

tempting _____

tender (verb) _____

discoveries

1. "Subliminal" and "sublime" look very similar, but they have very different meanings. Give a definition for them. What are their etymologies? What does "sublimate" mean?

2. The "subjunctive" mood is a verb form that is frequently misunderstood by inexperienced writers. Why, for example, do we say "I *was*..." but "If I *were*..., I would..."? What is the subjunctive? Contrast the subjunctive with the indicative and imperative moods.

3. What is the difference between "pertinent" and "impertinent"?

4. Distinguish the following words and phrases: ratio, ration, rational, rationale, rationalize, rational number, pro rata.

5. Define the following <u>fin</u> words and phrases: definitive, finality, fin-de-siècle, finesse, finite verb, fines herbes, finis, finitude, grand finality, infinitesimal, infinity.

6. What do "sensual," "sensory," and "sensuality" mean? Distinguish these words from "sexual" and "sexuality."

7. Define the following: ostensible, ostentation, ostentatious. How do the root parts of these words contribute to their meanings?

8. "Commemorative" coins are sometimes issued for world's fairs, royal coronations, Presidential inaugurations, and other special occasions. What are these coins? What is the etymology of "commemorative"?

9. Who was the Roman goddess Minerva? Connect her name to the <u>min</u> root.

10. According to some linguists, the informal term "nincompoop" contains a root found in this lesson. Consult various dictionaries for this purported etymology.

11. Distinguish the following <u>tain</u> words: abstain, attain, contain, detain, entertain, obtain, pertain, retain, appertain, sustain. How do the different prefixes used here help shape the meanings of the words?

12. "Minestrone" is a thick vegetable soup of Italian origin. Consult your dictionary for its very interesting etymology.

awakenings

The following words are formed from word roots introduced in this lesson and in previous ones. Consult your dictionary for words you are unsure of. Use this list to awaken your word sense and help you master this lesson.

abstain	intention	rationalize
admonish	irrational	refinement
attempt	joint	remembrance
attention	jugular	resent
attract	junta	retention
cohesive	limitation	sense
commemorative	memoir	sensor
comment	mentality	sentiment
conjunction	monitor	sentry
container	obtain	subtraction
contract	portrait	temptation
eliminate	preliminary	tenant
finale	pretense	tendency
finish	ratiocinative	tender
insensitive	rationale	traction

14   **roots**

Root Form	_Root Meaning_	_Examples_
1. **cub, cumb**	lie, hollow	**cub**ical, suc**cumb**
2. **dorm**	sleep/rest	**dorm**itory
3. **mod, med, mens**	style, measure, take measures	**mod**eration, **med**icate, di**mens**ion
4. **nihil, nil, nul(l)**	nothing	**nihil**ism, **nil**, **null**ify
5. **non-, ne-, neg-, neu-**	not, deny	**non**sensical, **neg**ative, **ne**farious, **neu**tral
6. **numer**	number	**numer**ous
7. **pau, pauc, pov**	few/little	**pau**per, **pauc**ity **pov**erty
8. **pend, pens**	pay, give	ex**pend**, dis**pens**e
9. **pend, pens, pond**	consider, hang	**pend**ing, **pens**ive, **pond**er
10. **scal, scan, scend, scent**	climb, step	**scal**e, **scan**sion, de**scend**, a**scent**
11. **somn**	sleep	in**somn**iac
12. **tot**	all, whole	**tot**alitarian

         root awakenings

notes

exercises

WORD ANALYSIS: Break each boldfaced word down to its basic parts and give a suitable definition for each part. Ignore suffixes not covered in lessons.

1. Herb stopped smoking for a week; then he **SUCCUMBED** to temptation.

2. **INSOMNIACS** are urged to avoid coffee, tea, and other forms of caffeine.

3. Lee **RENEGED** on her pledge to serve her whole term on the committee.

4. The labor agreement was **NULLIFIED** following the union's latest strike.

5. **INNUMERATES** are people unskilled in basic mathematical operations.

6. Streets that intersect one another at right angles are **PERPENDICULAR**.

7. Many **NONPRESCRIPTION** drugs can be purchased in grocery stores.

8. When we work hard, we ought to be **COMPENSATED** for our efforts.

9. Many Americans of Irish **DESCENT** dream of visiting Ireland one day.

10. **IMPONDERABLE** problems defy easy analysis or simple solutions.

MATCHING: Match the correct definition to the words listed below.

_____ ascendancy

_____ dormant

_____ incubus

_____ medicament

_____ modicum

_____ nihilism

_____ nil

_____ paucity

_____ pensive

_____ scansorial

A. inactive; idle; passive; lifeless

B. belief that the mind, soul, and body do not exist

C. evil spirit or force residing within an individual

D. rising; able to move in a vertical manner

E. superiority; advantage

F. treatment that promotes recovery from an injury

G. thoughtful; absorbed; engrossed in thought

H. small amount; dash, pinch, or trace of something

I. scarcity; shortage; need

J. empty; devoid of content; zero

BRIEFLY DEFINED: Give a short definition for the words listed below. Consult your dictionary for items you are unsure of.

cubicle_____

neuter_____

modulate_____

numerology_____

pauper_____

discoveries

1. What is a dormer window? Look up the etymology of "dormer." How is this style of window connected to the root meaning of <u>dorm</u>?

2. A teetotaler is an individual who refrains from drinking any alcoholic beverages. What is the curious etymology of this word?

3. A negligee is a woman's loose-fitting robe or dressing gown. How is this word pronounced? Link its etymology to its meaning.

4. Operas, musicals, and other large-scale dramatic works often employ supernumeraries in their productions. What sorts of acting roles would such people play?

5. In films and television shows depicting life in the old American West, outlaws were often called renegades. Some politicians today might be considered renegades even though they are not associated with criminal activity. Explain.

6. In order to maximize their enjoyment of plays, theatergoers must be willing to "suspend their disbelief." What does this term mean?

7. "Nihil obstat" is an official approval by the Roman Catholic Church that a book or artistic work contains no material that is damaging to faith or morals. How does the root makeup of this term suggest this meaning?

8. What is the difference between Arabic numbers and Roman numerals?

9. Cubism was an early twentieth-century style of painting and sculpture. Relate this artistic style to the root <u>cub</u>.

10. What is totalitarianism? How does this kind of political rule differ from authoritarianism? Which George Orwell novel described life under a totalitarian form of government?

11. Not surprisingly, the dormouse is a hibernating rodent. Explain.

12. Some traditional grammarians argue that double negatives like "They don't have no money" are actually positive statements. What might be the basis for such a judgment?

awakenings

The following words are formed from word roots introduced in this lesson and in previous ones. Consult your dictionary for words you are unsure of. Use this list to awaken your word sense and help you master this lesson.

accommodate	impoverished	nullify
annihilate	independent	numerator
append	innumerable	numerical
appendix	insomniac	pendulous
ascent	interdependent	pendulum
commodity	medical	poverty
compensate	medicinal	remediable
cubicle	meditate	remedy
descent	mode	scalable
dormitory	moderate	scansion
enumerate	modest	stipend
escalator	negativity	suspend
expense	neglect	suspension
immense	negotiate	totality
impend	neutral	transcendental

15   roots

Root Form	_Root Meaning_	_Examples_
1. **ann, en(n)**	year	**ann**ual, bi**enn**ial
2. **dia, di**	day	**dia**ry, **di**urnal
3. **dur**	lasting, hard	**dur**able
4. **ev**	age	medi**ev**al
5. **medi**	middle, near	im**medi**ate
6. **noc(t), nox**	night	**noc**turnal, equi**nox**
7. **press**	press	im**press**
8. **prim, prin, pri**	first, foremost	**prim**itive, **prin**ce, **pri**ority
9. **second**	second	**second**ary
10. **semi-**	half, partially	**semi**annual
11. **sesqui-**	one and a half	**sesqui**centennial
12. **temp, temper, tempor**	time, state/condition, moderation	**temp**est, **temper**ature, **tempor**ary

notes

exercises

WORD ANALYSIS: Break each boldfaced word down to its basic parts and give a suitable definition for each part. Ignore suffixes not covered in lessons.

1. We're planning a surprise party for my parents' 50th **ANNIVERSARY**.

2. At 26.2 miles, the marathon is the runner's ultimate **ENDURANCE** race.

3. The paramedic applied a **COMPRESS** on the wound to stop the bleeding.

4. Political parties hold **PRIMARY** elections to select their final candidates.

5. In dates, B.C. means "before Christ"; A.D. stands for **ANNO DOMINI**.

6. Around 1500 the **MEDIEVAL** period ended, and the Renaissance began.

7. Solly made a bad **IMPRESSION** at the interview and did not get the job.

8. The Golden Rule is a **PRINCIPLE** that we should all endeavor to live by.

9. Many department stores hold **SEMIANNUAL** sales in January and July.

10. Our ambassador called for an **IMMEDIATE** end to all acts of terrorism.

MATCHING: Match the correct definition to the words listed below.

_____ diurnal   A. elbow or knee position when slightly bent

_____ express   B. 18 inches in length

_____ indurate   C. exclude or hold down; control or restrain

_____ intemperate   D. callous; insensitive; stubborn; firmly fixed

_____ mediate   E. leading or most significant part or role

_____ noctule   F. occurring every 24 hours

_____ primacy   G. excessive; extreme; unreasonable

_____ repress   H. dependent upon; involving; acting through

_____ semiflexion   I. push or squeeze out, as juice from an orange

_____ sesquipedal   J. kind of bat, so named for its aversion to light

BRIEFLY DEFINED: Give a short definition for the words listed below. Consult your dictionary for items you are unsure of.

annualize _____

duress _____

perennial _____

principality _____

tempestuous _____

discoveries

1. Statisticians will sometimes refer to a "median" and an "average" point or value. What is the difference between these?

2. Some grammarians argue that "The news media plays an important role..." is incorrect and that the sentence should be phrased, "The news media play an important role...." Explain.

3. "Contemporary" is often used to mean 'modern.' Using the root parts that constitute this word, provide a more accurate definition.

4. The word "primer" can be pronounced two different ways, with each pronunciation having its own different meaning. Consult your dictionary for the two forms of this word.

5. What are the meanings of the following prim phrases: prima donna, primary care, primary color, prime meridian, prime number, prime rate, prime time, primrose path?

6. The French word root journ gives us the following English words: adjourn, journal, journalism, journey, journeyman, and sojourn. From what Latin root contained in this lesson does the French form journ derive?

7. Consult your dictionary for the unexpected etymology of "dismal."

8. "Second" denotes two things: a unit of time ("60 seconds") and an order of occurrence ("he finished second"). Consult your dictionary to determine which roots the two "seconds" come from? Which root does "second" come from in this sentence: Harold seconded the motion to investigate the club's finances"?

9. One way that economists gauge industrial output is to measure the production and consumption of "durable goods." What is meant by this?

10. What does "prioritize" mean? Make up a sentence containing this word.

11. Impressionism and expressionism were schools of art that achieved prominence in the late 19th and in the 20th centuries, respectively. What do the constituent parts of the two words reveal about their meanings?

12. What is the president pro tempore of the U. S. Senate?

awakenings

The following words are formed from word roots introduced in this lesson and in previous ones. Consult your dictionary for words you are unsure of. Use this list to awaken your word sense and help you master this lesson.

annals	impressionable	principality
anniversary	intermediary	principle
Anno Domini	longevity	prioress
annualize	media	priority
compress	mediate	repression
contemporary	medieval	secondary
depress	medium	semiannual
dial	nocturnal	semitrailer
diary	nocturne	suppress
durable	perennial	temperate
duress	primacy	temperature
endurance	primate	tempest
espresso	primer	tempo
expressive	prince	temporal
immediate	principal	temporary

16 roots

Root Form	Root Meaning	Examples
1. **bi-, bin-, bis-, du-**[†]	two	**bi**ped, **bin**oculars, **bis**cuit, **du**plex
2. **cent**	hundred, hundredth	**cent**ury
3. **dec**	ten, tenth	**dec**ade
4. **mill**	thousand, thousandth	**mill**igram
5. **non(a), nov(em)**	nine, ninth	**non**agon, **Novem**ber
6. **oct**	eight, eighth	**oct**ave
7. **quadr, quart, quatr**	four, fourth	**quadr**ant, **quart**er, **quatr**ain
8. **quin(t), quinqu**	five, fifth	**quint**uplet, **quinqu**ennial
9. **sept**	seven, seventh	**sept**et
10. **sex(t)**	six, sixth	**sext**et
11. **tri-, ter(t)-**	three, third	**tri**angle, **tert**iary
12. **un(i)-**	one	**uni**form

[†]**du-** and **bi-** come from different roots but are listed together because they share the same meaning.

notes

exercises

WORD ANALYSIS: Break each boldfaced word down to its basic parts and give a suitable definition for each part. Ignore suffixes not covered in lessons.

1. A **TRIDENT** is a spear or similar weapon so named because of its shape.

2. Jimmy Carter's presidency was a **QUADRENNIUM** of high inflation.

3. Doris's high grades put her in the top three **PERCENTILE** of her class.

4. 1992 was the **QUINCENTENNIAL** of Columbus's arrival to America.

5. **MILLIPEDES** are worm-like creatures with legs along their entire bodies.

6. Despite their campaign promises, politicians rarely **UNIFY** the country.

7. A **QUATRAIN** is a very short poem or a stanza of a longer poetic work.

8. Marcie was hoping for twins; she never imagined she'd have **TRIPLETS.**

9. The boiling point of water is 212° Fahrenheit or 100° **CENTIGRADE**.

10. If you **BISECT** a right angle, you end up with a pair of 45-degree angles.

MATCHING: Match the correct definition to the words listed below.

_____ bimanual   A. insignificant; not of major or primary importance

_____ bis   B. divided into twelve parts; a twelfth of the whole

_____ duodecimal   C. arranged in the corners and middle of a square

_____ nonagenarian   D. bringing together; combining; joining

_____ percentum   E. determined or controlled by a single gene

_____ quadrature   F. a person between the ages of 90 and 99

_____ quincuncial   G. in music, a direction to repeat a passage

_____ tertiary   H. a portion equal to $\frac{1}{100\text{th}}$ of the total

_____ unifactorial   I. requiring the use of both hands to operate

_____ unitive   J. process of making an area square or rectangular

BRIEFLY DEFINED: Give a short definition for the words listed below. Consult your dictionary for items you are unsure of.

dual_____

duel_____

milliard _____

tercentennial _____

unitary _____

discoveries

1. How long a period is a fortnight? a sennight? Look up their etymologies.

2. We often refer to useless or insignificant information as "trivia." How do the root parts of this word suggest this meaning?

3. What is the difference between "biannual," "biennial," and "semiannual"? To reduce confusion or misunderstanding, which of these words should you probably avoid using?

4. "Decimate" means to destroy a substantial amount of property or kill large numbers of people. Link its etymology to its original meaning.

5. What role did the triumvirate play in the governance of ancient Rome? What was the "decemvir"?

6. Some people use "unique" to mean 'very special or unusual.' Based on its etymology, this is an incorrect usage. Explain.

7. The decimal numbering system uses a base of ten; that is, it uses orderings or combinations of ten different numbers to express quantities. What is the base of a binary number system? How would you write the equivalences of the following numbers if you used a binary system: two, three, five, ten?

8. Tricorns were worn by men during the 18th century. What were they?

9. Etymologically speaking, September, October, November, and December are misnamed months. Explain.

10. How did the quarter horse get its name?

11. The U. S. Congress is a bicameral legislative body. What does this mean?

12. A million is one thousand thousands; a billion is one thousand thousand thousands or one thousand million; a trillion is one thousand thousand thousand thousands or one thousand billions. Put another way, a billion is 1,000 followed by two sets of "000," and a trillion is 1,000 followed by three sets of "000." What connection is there between the number and etymology of billion, trillion, quadrillion, etc.? How many zeroes are in a septillion, a nonillion, a decillion, and a centillion?

awakenings

The following words are formed from word roots introduced in this lesson and in previous ones. Consult your dictionary for words you are unsure of. Use this list to awaken your word sense and help you master this lesson.

bilingual	million	septet
binocular	nones	sesquicentennial
centennial	November	sexagenerian
centigrade	octave	tertiary
centipede	October	treble
centurion	percentage	tricentennial
century	quadratic	trinity
combine	quadruple	trio
December	quart	trivia
decimal	quarterly	unanimous
disunity	quatrain	union
dual	quint	unique
duplex	quintet	unitarian
duplicate	reunion	universal
millimeter	September	university

17   roots

Root Form	*Root Meaning*	*Examples*
1. acu, acr, acer(b), acid	sharp, point	**acu**te, **acr**imony, **acerb**ic, **acid**ity
2. alt, al, ol, ul	high, grow/grown, feed/support	**alt**itude, **al**imony, ab**ol**ish, ad**ul**t
3. apt, ept	fit, capable	**apt**itude, in**ept**
4. art, ert, arm	skill, capability, weapon	**art**istic, in**ert**, **arm**or
5. carn	meat, flesh	chili con **carn**e
6. don, dat, dit, dos, dot, dow	give	**don**or, **dat**ive, e**dit**, **dos**age, anec**dote**, en**dow**
7. -esce	becoming, growing	adol**esce**nt
8. hab(it), habil, hibit, ab(i)l, ib(i)l	have/hold, dwell, capable, suitable for	**habit**, re**habil**itate, ex**hibit**, pass**abl**e, imposs**ibil**ity
9. pecu	wealth, one's own	**pecu**liar
10. prehens, prehend	grab/seize	ap**prehend**, com**prehens**ive
11. priv, prop(e)r	lone, possess, loss/lack	**priv**ate, **prop**erty
12. vor	eat	carni**vor**e

notes

exercises

WORD ANALYSIS: Break each boldfaced word down to its basic parts and give a suitable definition for each part. Ignore suffixes not covered in lessons.

1. Wendy saw centuries-old **ARTIFACTS** in the archaeological museum.

2. The terrorists' bombing of the airport resulted in a grisly **CARNAGE**.

3. The warring factions finally signed an **ARMISTICE** that ended hostilities.

4. Many family members often take offense at Penny's **ACERBIC** sarcasm.

5. The new **EDITION** of the school yearbook will appear in several weeks.

6. Animals must **ADAPT** to their physical environment in order to survive.

7. Nineteenth-century **ABOLITIONISTS** worked to end slavery in the U.S.

8. With 8,000,000 **INHABITANTS**, New York is our most populous city.

9. California is **ENDOWED** with many natural resources and great beauty.

10. **COMPREHENSIVE** examinations cover all material covered in class.

MATCHING: Match the correct definition to the words listed below.

_____ aculeate		A. gradual reduction or lessening in force or strength
_____ appropriate		B. individual characteristics or traits of a person
_____ apt		C. in Roman law, property owned by a wife or child
_____ carnassial		D. impossible to satisfy; wanting more and more
_____ decrescendo		E. shared knowledge of a secret by several people
_____ habitus		F. take for one's individual benefit or use
_____ inert		G. describing the teeth of lions and similar animals
_____ peculium		H. equipped with a stinger, as with bees and wasps
_____ privity		I. sluggish; slow-moving; lazy; producing little
_____ voracious		J. expected; assumed; likely; probable

BRIEFLY DEFINED: Give a short definition for the words listed below. Consult your dictionary for items you are unsure of.

acuity_____

altimeter_____

habitual _____

omnivore _____

overdose _____

discoveries

1. How did the flower "carnation" derive its name?

2. Look up the etymology of "carnival." How is its original meaning connected to the Christian season of Lent?

3. Distinguish the following <u>art</u> words and phrases: artist, artiste, artisan, art deco, art nouveau, op art, pop art.

4. The word "prison" came about through a mispronunciation of a root introduced in this lesson. Consult your dictionary for this word's interesting etymology.

5. Some animals can be classified as apivorous, formicivorous, frugivorous, fungivorous, graminivorous, granivorous, herbivorous, insectivorous, piscivorous, seminivorous, and even vermivorous. What do these terms mean?

6. The college or university from which we graduate is our "alma mater." How do the root parts of this phrase metaphorically suggest its meaning?

7. Cultural and educational institutions rely on "endowments" to help pay their expenses. What is an endowment?

8. An "acid test" is a crucial test of the effectiveness or authenticity of something. What was this term's first meaning?

9. Certain plants and trees have "acerose" leaves. What does this term mean? Connect this meaning with the meaning of the root that makes up the word. Name a plant or tree whose leaves are acerose.

10. Many female singers have "alto" voices. What does this term mean? Look up the etymologies of these other voice types: soprano, mezzo-soprano, contralto, tenor, baritone, bass.

11. An anecdote is a little story that we might tell friends and colleagues. According to its etymology, however, it ought to be a passage that we should not be sharing. Explain.

12. A 1919 amendment to the U.S. Constitution was the Volstead Act, which began an era of American history whose name comes from a root introduced in this lesson. Name the root and this historical era.

awakenings

The following words are formed from word roots introduced in this lesson and in previous ones. Consult your dictionary for words you are unsure of. Use this list to awaken your word sense and help you master this lesson.

ability	armada	habitual
abolish	armament	incarnate
acidic	armory	incomprehensible
acrid	artificial	ineptitude
acumen	artisan	inertia
acute	carnal	omnivorous
adaptation	coalesce	peculiar
additive	cohabit	privacy
adolescence	crescent	privation
alarm	deprive	prohibit
alma mater	donor	prohibition
altar	dosage	proprietor
altitude	endow	reprehensible
apprehensive	exhibition	tradition
appropriate	habitat	voracity

Root Form	_Root Meaning_	_Examples_
1. **flu(v), fluct, flux**	flow	**flu**id, **fluct**uate, in**flux**
2. **fus, fund, found**	pour, melt/blend	in**fus**ion, re**fund**, con**found**
3. **lav, lu(v), lut, lug**	wash, pour	**lav**atory, e**luv**ium, pol**lut**e, de**lug**e
4. **plac, pleas**	please, calm	**plac**id, un**pleas**ant
5. **preci, prais**	worth, value	ap**preci**ate, **prais**e
6. **salu, salv, san**	health, mentally sound, clean, save, greet	**salu**tation, **salv**e, **san**itation
7. **sap, sip**	wise, taste	homo **sap**iens, in**sip**id
8. **sat**	fill/full	**sat**urate
9. **sci**	know, aware/feel	con**sci**entious
10. **simil, simul, simpl, sem(bl)**	same/alike, together, same form/time	**simil**ar, **simul**ate, **simpl**e, as**sembl**y
11. **spir, spri**	breathe, animate, struggle/endeavor	in**spir**ation, **spri**te
12. **vac, va(i)n, void**	empty, leave, vain, shun	**vac**ation, **van**ity, a**void**

notes

exercises

WORD ANALYSIS: Break each boldfaced word down to its basic parts and give a suitable definition for each part. Ignore suffixes not covered in lessons.

1. We were **DELUGED** with phone calls offering sympathy after the fire.

2. Some U.S. immigrants abandon their cultural roots and **ASSIMILATE**.

3. Paramedics administered artificial **RESPIRATION** to the accident victim.

4. Most Christians, Jews, and Muslims regard their God as **OMNISCIENT.**

5. Yesterday's fire alarm caused the public library to be **EVACUATED**.

6. Lake **PLACID**, New York, was the site of the 1980 Winter Olympics.

7. A new car will **DEPRECIATE** as soon as you drive it off the dealer's lot.

8. Henry's power was **DILUTED** when Julie was named the new president.

9. Rick's unexpected temper tantrums always **CONFOUNDED** his friends.

10. Dot has an **INSATIABLE** curiosity; she asks questions about everything.

MATCHING: Match the correct definition to the words listed below.

_____ affluent	A. capable; skillful; competent
_____ aurilave	B. cleansing of a body organ with water; an enema
_____ dissemble	C. stream that empties into a river; a tributary
_____ lavage	D. excess; oversupply; superabundance
_____ salvific	E. stupid; lacking intelligence or insight
_____ sanicle	F. pretense; empty display; false appearance
_____ satiety	G. brush or sponge used for cleaning the ear
_____ sciential	H. spiritually redeeming; bringing the soul to God
_____ semblance	I. disguise; conceal one's true nature or motives
_____ vacuous	J. flowering plant with medicinal qualities

BRIEFLY DEFINED: Give a short definition for the words listed below. Consult your dictionary for items you are unsure of.

appreciable_____

fusion _____

influx _____

placate _____

vacate _____

discoveries

1. A physician might prescribe a placebo to cure what is ailing us, especially if that malaise is "all in our head." Explain.

2. What is the difference between precious and semiprecious stones? Give an example of each.

3. "Appraise" and "apprise" are two verbs that speakers frequently mix up. How do these words differ in meaning? From what root, introduced in the previous lesson, does "apprise" derive? What does "apprize" mean?

4. The word "bedlam" refers to a place or situation full of confusion, noise, or chaos. Originally it was the name of an insane asylum. Consult your dictionary for this unusual connection.

5. Lava lamps were popular items during the 1950s. What were they?

6. A lavabo and a laver each have religious significance. Explain. In the "Awakenings" section of this lesson you'll find another word with a religious connection deriving from this root group. What is it? Define.

7. "Satire," which usually suggests an ironic or sarcastic take on a subject, derives from the sat root meaning 'fill/full.' Consult your dictionary for this word's original meaning and connection to its present-day meaning.

8. Define the following sci words and phrases: Christian Science, conscientious, conscious, pseudoscientific, science fiction, scientific method, scilicet, scire facias, sciolism.

9. A fax machine sends and receives pictures and documents over telephone lines. Look up its etymology and connect it to a root contained in this lesson.

10. What is a simile? Give an example of a simile.

11. Public television and radio stations sometimes simulcast programs. What does this mean?

12. An expired driver's license is no longer valid. How do the constituent parts of "expire" suggest this meaning? Based on this usage, what do you think was the original meaning of this word?

awakenings

The following words are formed from word roots introduced in this lesson and in previous ones. Consult your dictionary for words you are unsure of. Use this list to awaken your word sense and help you master this lesson.

affluence	fluency	sanity
antediluvian	influenza	sapor
appraisal	insipid	satiate
appreciation	lavatory	satisfaction
assemble	omniscience	savior
complacent	perspire	similitude
confusion	placate	simplex
conscientious	profuse	simplicity
conscious	resemblance	simulate
devastate	respirator	simultaneous
devoid	salutary	spiracle
dilution	salutatorian	spiritual
dissatisfied	salvage	sprite
evacuate	sanitary	vacancy
facsimile	sanitize	verisimilitude

19   **roots**

Root Form	*Root Meaning*	*Examples*
1. **cal, calor**	heat	**cal**dron, **calor**ie
2. **cand, cens, cend, cin(d), ciner**	fire/burn, white, glow/shine, ashes	**cand**le, in**cens**e, in**cend**iary, **cind**er, in**ciner**ator
3. **flam, flagr**	burn, blaze, bright	in**flam**e, **flagr**ant
4. **lud, lus**	play, deceive	e**lud**e, al**lus**ion
5. **lum(en), lumin, luc, lust(e)r**	light, clear, easily seen	**lumen**, **lumin**ary, **luc**id, il**lustr**ate
6. **mor(t)**	dead/death	**mort**uary
7. **nec, noc, nox, nuis**	harm	**nec**tar, in**noc**ent, **nox**ious, **nuis**ance
8. **pung, pug(n), punct, point**	fight, fist, pierce, point/mark	**pung**ent, im**pugn**, **punct**ual, ap**point**
9. **put**	reckon, suppose, cut	am**put**ate
10. **rupt**	burst, break	bank**rupt**
11. **sult, sa(i)l, sil, sau(l)t**	jump/leap, attack	re**sult**, **sal**mon, re**sil**ient, **saut**e
12. **val, vail**	good/well, farewell, strong, useful	**val**iant, a**vail**

notes

exercises

WORD ANALYSIS: Break each boldfaced word down to its basic parts and give a suitable definition for each part. Ignore suffixes not covered in lessons.

1. Restaurants often serve crêpes suzettes with a **FLAMBÉED** brandy sauce.

2. **NOCTILUCA** are marine plants that give water a shimmering appearance.

3. Motor oil reduces the **CALORIFACIENT** effects of friction in engines.

4. Arthritis, or **INFLAMMATION** of the joints, can be a painful condition.

5. A **DEPUTY** is someone appointed or authorized to act for another person.

6. Many cities use **INCINERATORS** to dispose of their garbage and waste.

7. **TRANSLUCENT** glass is used in bathroom windows to ensure privacy.

8. The retiring general gave a tearful **VALEDICTION** to his devoted troops.

9. We have but one **REPUTATION**; we should make sure it's a good one.

10. Smokers today use butane lighters; a century ago they had **LUCIFERS**.

MATCHING: Match the correct definition to the words listed below.

_____ candent   A. ornamental candle stick; torch

_____ cinerarium   B. evil influence/effect of the past on the present

_____ flambeau   C. glistening; reflecting; sparkling

_____ illuminati   D. chemical substance found in the tails of fireflies

_____ luciferin   E. brilliantly bright or white; ablaze

_____ ludic   F. assume former or original state; spring back

_____ mortmain   G. place for keeping remains of cremated bodies

_____ relucent   H. expression used when taking leave; good-bye

_____ resile   I. frollicking; not serious; joking

_____ vale   J. people claiming special knowledge or wisdom

BRIEFLY DEFINED: Give a short definition for the words listed below. Consult your dictionary for items you are unsure of.

caldron _____

invalid (adjective) _____

invalid (noun) _____

luminescence _____

sauté _____

discoveries

1. What is a mortgage? What does it mean to amortize a debt? How is the <u>mort</u> root figuratively related to the meanings of these words?

2. The <u>lud</u> root makes its way into several musical terms, especially those dealing with symphonic works and operas. Find the two musical <u>lud</u> terms listed in the "Awakenings" section of this lesson. Define them.

3. We usually associate calories with diet and body weight--a dish loaded with calories is fattening. Explain the connection between calories and the <u>calor</u> root's meaning of 'heat.'

4. Political candidates and ambition go hand in hand; that is, you rarely find the one without the other. In Lesson 5 ("Discoveries") you learned the original meaning of "ambition." Consult your dictionary for the surprising etymology of "candidate."

5. What is the difference between an allusion and an illusion?

6. "Nectar" and "nectarine" both derive from the <u>nec</u> root meaning 'harm.' Explain the curious connection between these two words and this root.

7. "Incense" is both a noun and a verb that, despite the common etymology, have different meanings and pronunciations. Distinguish them.

8. "Candid," which comes from the <u>cand</u> root, would appear to bear no relation to the root's meaning of fire/burn, white, etc. Explain this connection.

9. How do "flammable" and "inflammable" differ in meaning?

10. A number of c-e-n-s words in English are etymologically unrelated to the <u>cens</u> root in this lesson, including "censor," "censure," and "census." What do these words mean? From which Latin root do they derive?

11. What does the term "mortality rate" mean? Considering the fact that all of us must die eventually, how is it that some groups have higher mortality rates than do others?

12. High school graduation ceremonies often include an address by the valedictorian of the senior class. What is a "valedictorian"?

awakenings

The following words are formed from word roots introduced in this lesson and in previous ones. Consult your dictionary for words you are unsure of. Use this list to awaken your word sense and help you master this lesson.

abrupt	exult	luster
acupuncture	flamboyant	mortal
amortization	flamingo	mortician
assailant	illusion	obnoxious
bankrupt	illustrious	pointillism
calorific	impute	prelude
candela	incandescent	prevail
cinder	incense	punctilious
Cinderella	incorruptible	repugnant
collude	innocent	resilient
compunction	insult	salient
conflagration	interlude	sauté
devaluation	invaluable	somersault
disrupt	lumen	valence
equivalent	luminous	valuation

20   roots

Root *Form*	Root *Meaning*	*Examples*
1. **aqu**	water	**aqu**amarine
2. **cli, clin, cliv**	lean/tend toward, bed, support	**cli**ent, **clin**ician, pro**cliv**ity
3. **clud, clus, claus, clo(s), clois, clav**	close/shut/lock, key, settle, alone	in**clud**e, ex**clus**ion, **claus**trophobia, **clos**et, **clois**ter, **clav**ichord
4. **flor, flour, foli, foil**	flower, plant/growth, leaf, sheet	**flor**ist, **flour**, **foli**age, air**foil**
5. **lat**	carry/bear, bring	re**lat**e
6. **lat, later**	side, wide, support	**lat**itude, col**later**al
7. **lig, li(a), ly, loy,**	bind, connect	**lig**ament, **lia**ison, re**ly**, **loy**alty
8. **misc, mix**	mix	**misc**ellaneous, **mix**ture
9. **moll**	soft	**moll**ify
10. **par, per**	beget, produce	**par**ent, re**per**tory
11. **ter(r)**	earth, ground	**ter**ritory
12. **vuls**	pull, shake	con**vuls**ion

notes

exercises

WORD ANALYSIS: Break each boldfaced word down to its basic parts and give a suitable definition for each part. Ignore suffixes not covered in lessons.

1. I had to work and was forced to **DECLINE** Garth's invitation to dinner.

2. The U.S. and Japan began **BILATERAL** talks to ease the trade dispute.

3. **MULTIPAROUS** animal species bear two or more offspring at one time.

4. In the summer we enjoy **AQUATIC** sports like swimming and boating.

5. Chemical **DEFOLIANTS** are used to clear away forest area and brush.

6. Military combat vehicles are designed for **SUBAQUEOUS** operation.

7. Nick **RELATES** well with young people; he should become a teacher.

8. Scandanavians toast one another with a strong drink called **AQUAVIT.**

9. The **RECLUSE** Howard Hughes avoided publicity most of his adult life.

10. Despite his promises George felt no **OBLIGATION** to finish the job.

MATCHING: Match the correct definition to the words listed below.

_____ aquifer

_____ cloistral

_____ conclave

_____ declivitous

_____ florescence

_____ latitudinarian

_____ liana

_____ milfoil

_____ mollify

_____ terrene

A. secret meeting; gathering in a secret place

B. productive period of success or achievement

C. tropical vine that climbs and clings to trees

D. hidden from view; situated away from; by oneself

E. underground stream or source of water

F. worldly; of a region or land

G. steep; sloping downward; going down hill

H. soothe; lighten; lessen in intensity

I. tolerant person who accepts different opinions

J. type of thick bushy plant found along roadsides

BRIEFLY DEFINED: Give a short definition for the words listed below. Consult your dictionary for items you are unsure of.

Aquarius_____

circulate _____

elate_____

extraterrestrial _____

superlative _____

discoveries

1. "Dilate" is a word most of us know; it means to expand or grow bigger, as with the pupils of our eyes. Which <u>lat</u> root does this word derive from? Consult your dictionary for "dilatory," which looks very much like "dilate" but comes from the other <u>lat</u> root. What does this word mean?

2. In 1492 Christopher Columbus sailed the seas for months before finally hitting terra firma. What is "terra firma"? What do these other <u>terr</u> words and phrases mean: terra cotta, terra incognita, terrazzo, terrestrial planet, territorial waters?

3. Define the following <u>mix</u> phrases: mixed bag, mixed doubles (in tennis), mixed drink, mixed grill, mixed marriage, mixed media, mixed metaphor.

4. "Liable" is commonly used to mean 'likely' or 'expected to happen.' Does your dictionary accept this usage? Explain.

5. "Closure" denotes the curtailing or closing up of something, be it a factory, an event, or a flesh wound. How does this word differ from "cloture"?

6. While no mammal species is oviparous, most are multiparous. What do these <u>par</u> words mean?

7. Name three species of animals that are mollusks. Why are these creatures so-named? What is a crustacean?

8. What is automobile liability insurance? Link it to the <u>lig</u> root.

9. Define and distinguish the following <u>flor</u>-related words: cinquefoil, foil, folio, floriculture, florid, floriferous, flourish. How would you explain the connection between the <u>flor</u> root and "flour."

10. The clavicle is the collarbone in humans and other primates. Why is this bone so-named? What is the connection between "clavicle" and the <u>clav</u> root?

11. The portfolio you would expect a commercial artist to have is very different from the portfolio a stock investor might own. Explain.

12. Automobile safety experts might inform us that gasoline and alcohol are immiscible. What message would they be sending us?

awakenings

The following words are formed from word roots introduced in this lesson and in previous ones. Consult your dictionary for words you are unsure of. Use this list to awaken your word sense and help you master this lesson.

ablative	flora	oblige
alloy	Florida	parental
ally	foliage	parterre
Aquarius	folio	portfolio
circulate	intermix	preclude
clause	lateral	promiscuous
clavier	legislature	recluse
collateral	liaison	reliance
conclusive	lien	seclude
convulse	loyalist	superlative
decline	Mediterranean	terrace
defoliate	miscellany	terrain
disclosure	mollify	terrier
emollient	mollusk	territory
equilateral	multilateral	translation

greek word roots

roots

Root Form	*Root Meaning*	*Examples*
1. a-, an-	not/without	**ap**athy, **an**archy
2. and(e)r	male	phil**ander**
3. anthrop	human	**anthrop**ology
4. bi(o)	life	**bio**sphere
5. cent(e)r	center	**centr**ifugal
6. en(do)-, em-	in	**en**zyme, **em**pathy
7. ge(o)	earth	**geo**grapher
8. gram, graph	write, record	tele**gram**, **graph**ic
9. gyn(ec)	woman/female	**gynec**ologist
10. log	idea, word, speech, reason, study	eu**log**y
11. mis(o)-	hate	**mis**anthrope
12. -oid	resembling/like	human**oid**
13. path	disease, feel	psycho**path**ic
14. phil	love, attracted to	**Phil**adelphia
15. syn-, sym-, syl-, sy-	together/with	**syn**thetic, **sym**bol, **syl**lable, **sy**stematic

notes

exercises

WORD ANALYSIS: Break each boldfaced word down to its basic parts and give a suitable definition for each part. Ignore suffixes not covered in lessons.

1. Many scientists believe a state of **ABIOSIS** exists on the moon's surface.

2. **PHILANTHROPISTS** are famous for their large donations to charity.

3. The theater's circular stage was ringed by **CONCENTRIC** rows of seats.

4. Student **APATHY** is the greatest challenge facing today's school teachers.

5. **PHILOLOGISTS** specialize in the historical development of languages.

6. Hartley always loves reading **BIOGRAPHIES** when she is on vacation.

7. A **SYLLOGISM** is a mode of reasoning that relies upon deductive logic.

8. The **GEOID** is the imaginary surface of our planet that exists at sea level.

9. **GRAPHOLOGISTS** assign personality traits to a person's handwriting.

10. A triangle's **CENTROID** is the point at which its three median lines meet.

MATCHING: Match the correct definition to the words listed below.

_____ andron   A. distrust of reason, logical processes, or science

_____ agraphia   B. a Casanova- or Don Juan-type individual; a rake

_____ endobiota   C. mutually beneficial relationship between persons

_____ geocentrism   D. in ancient Greece, a banquet hall for men

_____ geoponic   E. a brain disorder that causes an inability to write

_____ gynecoid   F. belief that the sun revolves around the earth

_____ logogram   G. symbolic representation of a word

_____ misology   H. parasites; creatures residing within a host animal

_____ philogynist   I. not masculine; having female characteristics

_____ symbiosis   J. pertaining to farming or planting; agricultural

BRIEFLY DEFINED: Give a short definition for the words listed below. Consult your dictionary for items you are unsure of.

bionic_____._____

centralize_____

grammatical_____

syllogism_____

sympathy_____

discoveries

1. In some words the <u>and(e)r</u> root denotes 'maleness' in humans, but in many others it is used for other species, especially flowers. Which of the following <u>and(e)r</u> words refer to humans, to nonhumans, or to both: androgen, diandrous, holandric, misandry, monandrous, monandry, pachysandra?

2. What is the difference between an android and an anthropoid?

3. Define these additional <u>-oid</u> words: adenoid, alkaloid, amoeboid, asteroid, dendroid, dentoid, ellipsoid, factoid, hemorrhoid, hysteroid, ichthyoid, ovoid, paranoid, rheumatoid, schizoid, steroid, thyroid, toxoid, trapezoid, zooid.

4. What do the following <u>-centric</u> words mean: acrocentric, anthropocentric, concentric, eccentric, egocentric, ethnocentric, geocentric, heliocentric, homocentric, polycentric, telocentric, theocentric?

5. What is the difference between a geographer and a geologist?

6. Distinguish a sympathetic person from someone who is empathetic.

7. In the 17th century Quaker settlers were among those who established the city of Philadelphia, Pa. What is the etymology of this city's name?

8. Neanderthal man is an early, extinct member of the species homo sapiens, to which modern humans belong. Despite the word's 'ander' sequence, it does not derive directly from the Greek <u>ander</u> root. What is its etymology?

9. Compare the meanings of the <u>log</u> root in the following words: analogy, biology, catalogue, chronology, doxology, logic, neologism, pathology.

10. Distinguish the following <u>mis(o)</u>- words: misanthropic, misocainea, misogamy, misogynist, misoneist, misopedia.

11. What is philately? What is its etymology? What is the difference between a philatelist and a numismatist? What is a phillumenist?

12. Consult your dictionary for the definitions of these <u>-phile</u> words: acidophile, ailurophile, Anglophile, audiophile, bibliophile, cinephile, Francophile, halophile, homophile, necrophile, Russophile, thermophile.

awakenings

The following words are formed from word roots introduced in this lesson as well as in Latin lessons . Consult your dictionary for words you are unsure of. Use this list to awaken your word sense and help you master this lesson.

agraphic	decentralize	logogram
androgen	digraph	misanthropy
androgynous	egocentricity	misogynous
android	empathic	pathetic
anthropoid	endobiotic	pathogen
apathetic	endogenous	pathology
audiogram	factoid	pathos
biocidal	flexography	philology
biogenic	geocentric	program
biome	geoid	sociopath
bioscience	geological	sonogram
biosensor	geoponic	syllogistic
centigram	grammatical	sympathize
centrist	grapheme	syncline
concentric	hominoid	videophile

22   **roots**

<u>Root</u> <u>Form</u>	<u>Root</u> <u>Meaning</u>	<u>Examples</u>
1. **ana-**	back/again, up/upon	**ana**logy
2. **ant(i)-**	against	**anti**climactic
3. **aut(o)-, taut(o)-**	self, same	**autos, tauto**logy
4. **chrom(at)**	color	**chrom**ium
5. **chron**	time	**chron**ic
6. **-crat, -cracy**	rule/govern	demo**crat**, bureau**cracy**
7. **dem**	people	**dem**ography
8. **dia-**	through, across	**dia**logue
9. **mani(a)**	madness, mad desire	klepto**mania**
10. **ne(o)**	new	**neo**conservative
11. **onym, onom(at)**	name	pseud**onym**, **onomat**opoeia
12. **phob**	fear/dread	acro**phob**ia
13. **phon**	sound	**phon**etics
14. **scop, skep**	examine	horo**scop**e, **skep**tic
15. **tel(e)-**	distant/far	**tele**vision

notes

exercises

WORD ANALYSIS: Break each boldfaced word down to its basic parts and give a suitable definition for each part. Ignore suffixes not covered in lessons.

1. Zak's all-time favorite book is Benjamin Franklin's **AUTOBIOGRAPHY**.

2. Roy claims that he can communicate with ancestors using **TELEPATHY**.

3. Doctors administer **ANTIDOTES** to patients who have swallowed poison.

4. Teachers used to make their pupils **DIAGRAM** sentences in English class.

5. Two words having the same or similar meaning are called **SYNONYMS**.

6. In **DEMOCRACIES** all citizens may participate in the political process.

7. Some books nowadays are ghostwritten, but most are **AUTONYMOUS**.

8. An **ANALOGY** is a likening or comparison of things that are dissimilar.

9. The Hubble Space **TELESCOPE** explores the heavens as it orbits Earth.

10. A **SYMPHONY** is a musical work having distinct movements or sections.

MATCHING: Match the correct definition to the words listed below.

_____ anonym   A. historical change; development over many years

_____ asynchronous   B. foghorn having a low-pitched, penetrating signal

_____ autocide   C. alias; assumed or false name

_____ diachrony   D. out of control; agitated; frantic

_____ diaphone   E. operating apart from; not coincident with

_____ endemic   F. set of rules governing a language's pronunciation

_____ manic   G. killing oneself by causing a motor vehicle crash

_____ misoneistic   H. related to species of modern human beings

_____ neanthropic   I. native to; belonging to a specific place or group

_____ phonology   J. resistant to change; desiring the established order

BRIEFLY DEFINED: Give a short definition for the words listed below. Consult your dictionary for items you are unsure of.

analogous _____

automaton _____

chromatic_____

chronicle_____

telescopic_____

discoveries

1. Each year the music recording industry honors its top artists with grammy awards. "Grammy" is an abbreviation for what word? What two Greek roots are found in the unabbreviated form of grammy?

2. The <u>onym</u> root, which usually functions as a suffix, is a very productive form that appears in dozens of English words. Consult your dictionary for the meanings of these: allonym, homonym, metonymy, metronymic, patronymic, tautonym, toponymic.

3. Baptists make up the largest Protestant denomination in America. A sect not connected to American Baptism is Anabaptism. What do its followers believe? Relate the <u>ana-</u> root to the meaning of Anabaptism.

4. You are probably familiar with these words ending in the -<u>cracy</u> suffix: aristocracy, democracy. Consult your dictionary for those you don't know. How many of these -<u>cracy</u> words do you know: hagiocracy, kakistocracy, kleptocracy, meritocracy, mobocracy, narcokleptocracy, ochlocracy, plutocracy, slavocracy, stratocracy, thalassocracy, timocracy?

5. We read that our national and state capitals are full of "bureaucrats." What does this term mean? What negative meaning is often attached to this word?

6. Compact discs or CDs are digitally recorded, while LPs are analog recordings. Relate the word "analog" to the production of music records.

7. What is the difference between a geographer and a demographer?

8. In most words in which it appears, the Latin root <u>agr(i)</u> carries the meaning of 'field' or 'farming' (e.g. agrarian, agribusiness, agriculture). How does this root's meaning change in this <u>mania</u> word: agromania?

9. What is manic depression? Relate it to the <u>manic</u> root.

10. "Bang," "creak," "sizzle," and "slurp" are all examples of onomatopoeia. What does this word mean? How do its root parts suggest its meaning?

11. A skeptic is a "doubting Thomas" who always demands proof. What is the word history of "doubting Thomas"? Who were the Skeptics?

12. Antarctica is the southernmost continent. What is its etymology?

awakenings

The following words are formed from word roots introduced in this lesson and in previous ones. Consult your dictionary for words you are unsure of. Use this list to awaken your word sense and help you master this lesson.

achromatic	chromatic	maniac
anachronism	chromatography	neanthropic
anagram	chronic	neogenesis
analog	chronology	neology
anonym	chromoscope	onomastic
antibiotic	claustrophobia	patronymic
anticline	democratic	phonate
antigen	demographer	phonograph
antiphonal	diachronic	phonoscope
antisocial	dialog	symphony
asynchronous	dichromatic	synchronize
autobiographical	egomaniacal	synonymous
autocrat	endemic	telepathy
autograph	geochronology	televise
bioscopy	gynecocracy	video phone

Root Form	Root Meaning	Examples
1. **arch, archa(e)**	rule, first, foremost	**arch**angel, **archa**ic
2. **ast(e)r**	star, heavens	**astr**ology
3. **cac(o)-**	bad/badly	**caco**phonous
4. **cosm**	universe/world, order	**cosm**onaut
5. **ec, ect(o)-, ex(o)-**	out of, outside	**ec**static, **ecto**zoic, **exo**tic
6. **eco**	household, environment	**eco**system
7. **eu-**	good, genuine	**eu**phemism
8. **hier(o)**	holy/sacred	**hiero**glyphics
9. **-lat(e)r**	worship	icono**latr**y
10. **manc, mant**	prophesy	astro**manc**y, praying **mant**is
11. **met(e)r**	measure	kilo**meter**
12. **morph**	shape/form	meta**morph**osis
13. **nom**	system, law	gastro**nom**y
14. **peri-**	around	**peri**scope
15. **tax, tact**	arrange/arrangement	syn**tax**, **tact**ics

notes

exercises

WORD ANALYSIS: Break each boldfaced word down to its basic parts and give a suitable definition for each part. Ignore suffixes not covered in lessons.

1. Christians utilize many **HIEROGRAMS**, including the fish and the cross.

2. Sentries patrolled the **PERIMETER** of the base camp looking for snipers.

3. Biology majors must take courses in plant and animal **MORPHOLOGY**.

4. We ignore Douglas's **ECCENTRICITIES** because he has a heart of gold.

5. Thousands of **ASTEROIDS** circle the sun near the orbital path of Mars.

6 The party **HIERARCHY** planned the campaign strategy for the election.

7. Carlton is an **EGOMANIAC**; he always has to be the center of attention.

8. Submarines use **PERISCOPES** to spot the exact location of enemy ships.

9. The Federal Reserve Bank closely monitors the nation's **ECONOMY**.

10. Manny's **EULOGY** at Earl's funeral was an emotionally charged speech.

MATCHING: Match the correct definition to the words listed below.

_____ anomie   A. convert to the decimal or similarly based system

_____ autarch   B. relating to priests and their religious activities

_____ bionomics   C. tyrant; authoritarian ruler; cruel dictator

_____ caconym   D. close to the time of birth or origin of an organism

_____ ectomorphic   E. ecological balance; environmental influence

_____ exobiota   F. erroneous or faulty name or label; a misnomer

_____ geotaxis   G. movement that is determined by earth's gravity

_____ hieratic   H. absence or breakdown of order or rules in society

_____ metricize   I. creatures from outer space; extraterrestrial beings

_____ perinatal   J. having a thin body build; slight in appearance

BRIEFLY DEFINED: Give a short definition for the words listed below. Consult your dictionary for items you are unsure of.

cacophonous_____

cosmos _____

exotic_____

syntactic _____

trimeter _____

discoveries

1. Many animal species have exoskeletons while others have endoskeletons. What are these?

2. Deuteronomy is the fifth book of the Old Testament, although its etymology has nothing to do with its location in the Bible. Consult your dictionary for the meaning of the deutero root. What does the etymology of Deuteronomy suggest about this Old Testament book?

3. Despite its root makeup, astrology is not the scientific study of the stars. What is astrology? What is the meaning and etymology of "zodiac"?

4. We all complain about the high cost of things. What do we mean when we say that prices are "astronomically" high? Connect the roots of "astronomic" to its metaphorical meaning of 'extremely expensive.'

5. The religions of many cultures deal with issues of cosmogony. Explain.

6. The -latry suffix means 'worship of.' Define the following: bibliolatry, hagiolatry, iconolatry, idolatry, Mariolatry, zoolatry.

7. Our endocrine system secretes hormones and other fluids into our bodies. What is the function of exocrine glands? Name an exocrine gland.

8. Based on its etymology, what was the original meaning of "disaster"?

9. A geographer charts physical features and human populations on the earth. What would a cosmographer do?

10. Distinguish the following eu- words: eucalyptus, Eucharist, eudemon, eupepsia, euphemism, euphony, euphoria, eurhythmy, eustasy.

11. Appending the caco- prefix to roots usually has the opposite effect of adding the eu- prefix. Compare, for example, cacophony and euphony. What do these caco- words mean: cacoëthes, cacography, caconym?

12. Human societies have historically resorted to various means to foretell the future. Look up the following -mancy words for some of them: bibliomancy, chiromancy, geomancy, hydromancy, necromancy, oneiromancy, pyromancy, rhabdomancy.

awakenings

The following words are formed from word roots introduced in this lesson and in previous ones. Consult your dictionary for words you are unsure of. Use this list to awaken your word sense and help you master this lesson.

amorphous	cosmology	hieratic
anarchy	disastrous	mantis
anthropomorphic	eccentricity	metrication
archaic	econometrics	metrification
archivist	ecospecies	metronome
astral	eugenics	morphogenesis
astrobiology	eulogize	morphology
astrology	euphony	nomograph
astronomer	exarch	patriarchy
ataxic	exobiological	pedometer
autonomy	exogenous	perimeter
cacography	exotic	periscope
cacophonous	geomancy	symmetrical
cosmetologist	gynarchy	syntax
cosmography	hierarchy	telemetry

roots

Root *Form*	Root *Meaning*	*Examples*
1. **card**	heart	**card**iology
2. **cephal**[†]	head	micro**cephal**y
3. **chem**	substance, chemical	bio**chem**istry
4. **chir**	hand	**chir**opractor
5. **derm(at)**	skin	**dermat**ologist
6. **ep(i)-**	upon, over, after, also	**epi**center
7. **hem(at), em**	blood	**hem**orrage, an**em**ia
8. **iatr**	medical treatment	psych**iatr**ic
9. **-itis**	inflammation	tonsill**itis**
10. **phys**	nature, medical, material	**phys**ician
11. **pod, pus**	foot	tri**pod**, octo**pus**
12. **psych**	mind, spirit/soul	**psych**ology
13. **(r)rh, rhe(o)**	flow, stream/rush	**rh**ythmic, **rheo**stat
14. **som(at)**	body	chromo**som**e
15. **therap**	medical treatment	**therap**eutic

[†]**encephal** (**en** 'in' + **cephal** 'head') means 'brain'

notes

exercises

WORD ANALYSIS: Break each boldfaced word down to its basic parts and give a suitable definition for each part. Ignore suffixes not covered in lessons.

1. Doctors prescribed **BIBLIOTHERAPY** to help lessen Dan's depression.

2. **PSYCHOSOMATIC** disease is often harder to treat than other ailments.

3. Squids and **OCTOPUSES** are fearsome-looking denizens of the oceans.

4. Eczema, seborrhea, and psoriasis are all serious types of **DERMATITIS**.

5. Nate suffers from chronic **ANEMIA** and is under a doctor's constant care.

6. **PHYSIOLOGY** deals with the organic functions and parts of living things.

7. Many kinds of cancer are effectively controlled by **CHEMOTHERAPY**.

8. **HEMORRHOIDS** are often treated medically but may require surgery.

9. **ENCEPHALITIS** can be life-threatening if left to go without treatment.

10. The hospital's **PSYCHIATRIC** ward was located in a lovely forest area.

MATCHING: Match the correct definition to the words listed below.

_____ antipodean   A. living close to the ground, as surface vegetation

_____ cephalopod   B. instrument for determining fluid flow, esp. blood

_____ chiromancy   C. membrane that surrounds the human heart

_____ chronotherapy   D. a deep-red iron-containing pigment

_____ epigeal   E. the art and science of palm reading

_____ heme   F. species of mollusk that includes the octopus

_____ pericardium   G. situated diametrically opposite on the globe

_____ psychomancy   H. altering of normal sleeping hours to treat insomnia

_____ rheometer   I. belief that all mental illness has a physical origin

_____ somatism   J. communication between souls or with spirits

BRIEFLY DEFINED: Give a short definition for the words listed below. Consult your dictionary for items you are unsure of.

antidiarrheal _____

cardiogram _____

epidermis _____

hemorrhage _____

psyche _____

discoveries

1. What is the difference between an epigram and an epigraph?

2. Among the lesser known or less conventional medical treatments are the following: aerotherapy, aromatherapy, aversion therapy, bibliotherapy, biotherapy, chrysotherapy, organotherapy, primal therapy, and release therapy. How many of these could you guess the meanings of?

3. Distinguish a psychiatrist from a psychologist. What is the difference in their professional training?

4. The dictionary lists dozens of psychology specializations: Distinguish the following psychology types: abnormal, child, clinical, cognitive, comparative, depth, developmental, dynamic, educational, ego, experimental, gestalt, industrial, mass.

5. What is the meaning of the following "psych-" terms: psychoacoustics, psychobabble, psychedelic, psychodrama, psycholinguistics, psychopathic, psycho technics?

6. How many of the following -itis terms can you identify without a dictionary: arteritis, arthritis, bronchitis, colitis, gastritis, gingivitis, hepatitis, laryngitis, mastitis, retinitis, rhinitis, sinusitis, stomatitis? Consult your dictionary for -itis terms you could not identity.

7. What does a chiropractor do? Relate its constituent parts to its meaning.

8. The word "chromosome" literally means 'color + body.' Give a definition of the word. What is its function in the transference of hereditary characteristics among blood relatives.

9. What do the medical abbreviations EEG and EKG stand for?

10. What kinds of animals make up the following -pod species: Apoda, Arthropoda, Gastropoda, Myriapoda, Sauropoda?

11. What does psychosis mean? What does the -osis suffix often mean when appended to the following roots: aden-, alkol-, arthr-, chlor-, cirrh-, cyan-, dermat-, halit-, kerat-, melan-, neur-, thromb-.

12. What types of medical treatment are the following iatr words concerned with: bariatrics, geriatrics, pediatrics, physiatrics, podiatry, psychiatry?

awakenings

The following words are formed from word roots introduced in this lesson and in previous ones. Consult your dictionary for words you are unsure of. Use this list to awaken your word sense and help you master this lesson.

anemic	dermatoid	phonocardiogram
anencephaly	encephalitis	physiology
Antipodes	endoderm	physiotherapy
astrochemistry	epicardial	physique
astrophysics	epicenter	podiatry
autosome	epidemiology	podium
biochemistry	epidermis	psychochemical
biotherapy	epigram	psychogenic
cardiography	eponym	psychosomatic
centrosome	hematologist	psychotic
cephalometry	hemophilia	rheostat
chemosensory	hemorrhage	rheum
chemotaxis	hemostasis	somatotherapy
chirography	pathophysiology	symphysis
chiropodist	pericarditis	taxidermy

roots

Root Form	*Root Meaning*	*Examples*
1. **ap(o)-**	back, again, up/upon	**apo**logy
2. **dox**	belief	para**dox**
3. **dys-**	bad/badly	**dys**functional
4. **erg, urg**	work	en**erg**y, metall**urg**y
5. **hetero-**	different	**hetero**sexual
6. **hom(e)o-**	same/alike	**homo**genize
7. **macro-**	large	**macro**economics
8. **mega(lo)-**	great/very large	**megalo**maniac
9. **micro-**	small	**micro**scopic
10. **ops, op(t)**	eye, sight, examine	bi**ops**y, **opt**ician
11. **stat, stas**	stop/stand	**stat**ic, ec**stas**y
12. **therm**	heat	**therm**ostat
13. **thes, the(t)**	put/place	**thes**is, epi**thet**
14. **tom**[†]	cut	ana**tom**y
15. **zo(o)**	animal	proto**zoa**

[†]**ectom** (**ec** 'out of' + **tom** 'cut') means 'surgical removal'

notes

exercises

WORD ANALYSIS: Break each boldfaced word down to its basic parts and give a suitable definition for each part. Ignore suffixes not covered in lessons.

1. **ERGOGRAPHS** gauge the strength of muscles under stress or contraction.

2. Cheerleaders use **MEGAPHONES** to boost school spirit at football games.

3. A **SYNOPSIS** is a brief summary or overview of a book, story, or article.

4. A **MACROBIOTIC** diet consists mainly of whole grains and beans.

5. **CHEMURGY** develops new industrial products from organic materials.

6. **GEOTHERMAL** forces cause geysers to spew steam from the ground.

7. Paramedics gave Joe **HEMOSTATIC** drugs at the scene of the accident.

8. Because of the diversity, college campuses are cultural **MICROCOSMS**.

9. The **DOXOLOGY** is a hymn sung in many Christian worship services.

10. **APOSTASY** is the abandoning of one's religious beliefs and principles.

MATCHING: Match the correct definition to the words listed below.

_____ antithetical   A. organism's ability to maintain internal equilibrium

_____ azoic   B. words spelled alike but pronounced differently

_____ dysgenic   C. condition of balance or equilibrium; immobility

_____ dysgraphia   D. denoting geologic era before appearance of life

_____ entozoa   E. agreeing with; taking the same point of view

_____ heteronyms   F. causing deterioration of hereditary qualities

_____ homeostasis   G. exactly opposite of; in direct contrast to

_____ megalomanic   H. tapeworms and other similar parasites

_____ stasis   I. feeling or believing that one is totally powerful

_____ synoptic   J. inability to write due to a brain impairment

BRIEFLY DEFINED: Give a short definition for the words listed below. Consult your dictionary for items you are unsure of.

biopsy _____

dysfunctional _____

energize _____

microbe _____

zoology _____

discoveries

1. The term "apocryphal," which means 'not true or authentic,' derives from apo- ('away') and cryph (hide); thus, an apocryphal story should not be believed. What does the term " Apocrypha" mean to Bible scholars?

2. Some organisms are macroscopic, while others are microscopic. What is the difference between these terms?

3. Three astronomical terms that begin with the ap(o)- prefix are aphelion, apogee, and apolune. Distinguish them.

4. The -ectomy suffix, meaning 'surgical removal,' is a very productive word-building unit in English. "Appendectomy," for example, is familiar to all of us. Consult your dictionary for the definitions of these less commonly used -ectomy words: adenectomy, colectomy, craniectomy, embryectomy, gingivectomy, keratectomy, lipectomy, pneumonectomy, sympathectomy.

5. The scientific study of insects is called entomology. How do the constituent parts of "insect," which derives from Latin, and Greek-based "entomology" connect these two words?

6. Distinguish the meaning difference between Latin dis- and Greek dys-?

7. Consult your dictionary for the meanings of the following dys- words: dysentery, dyslexia, dyspepsia, dysrhythmia, dystopia, dystrophy.

8. The evolution and development of certain animal forms was important in dating the earth's prehistory. Look up the following -zoic words denoting certain geological eras and arrange them in chronological order: Archeozoic, Cenozoic, Mesozoic, Paleozoic, Proterozoic.

9. The cooling capacity of air conditioners is measured in B.T.U.'s. What exactly is a B.T.U.? What root from this lesson is contained in this term?

10. What is an optical illusion? A phrase akin to this term is the French phrase "trompe l'oeil." Consult your dictionary for its meaning and pronunciation.

11. What is an epithet? Link its present-day meaning to its etymology.

12. Considering the fact that nuclear energy is a reality today, why are the words "atom" and "atomic" etymologically misnamed?

awakenings

The following words are formed from word roots introduced in this lesson and in previous ones. Consult your dictionary for words you are unsure of. Use this list to awaken your word sense and help you master this lesson.

antithetical	ecstatic	macron
apochromatic	ectotherm	macroscopic
apophysis	erg	megalomania
apostasy	ergometric	megaphone
astasia	heterodoxy	microeconomic
bioenergetics	heterogeneous	microsome
biopsy	heterogenous	optician
cardiomegaly	heterotic	optometry
chemurgy	homeopathy	synergy
dermatome	homocentric	synoptic
doxology	homogenize	ultra micrometer
dysgenesis	homophone	zoogenous
dysgenics	homophobia	zooid
dysphonic	macrocosm	zoomorphic
eccentricity	macroeconomics	zootomy

26 roots

Root Form	_Root Meaning_	_Examples_
1. ac(m)-, acro-	top/summit, sharp, extremity/tip	**acm**e, **acro**phobia
2. agog	teach/instruct, induce	syn**agog**ue
3. bibl(io)	book	**biblio**phile
4. cycl	circle, wheel	bi**cycl**e
5. drom	run, course	**drom**edary
6. heli(o)	sun	**helio**centric
7. hydr	water, liquid	**hydr**aulic
8. hyp(o)-	under/below, partial	**hypo**dermic
9. hyper-	over/above, more than	**hyper**bole
10. lys, lyt, -lyz	break down, loosen	analy**sis**, cata**lyt**ic, para**lyz**e
11. ped	child, training/education	**ped**agogy
12. pyr(o)	fire	**pryo**maniac
13. soph	wise/wisdom	**soph**istocated
14. tech(n)	art/skill, build	**techn**ology
15. the(o)	god	a**the**ism

notes

exercises

WORD ANALYSIS: Break each boldfaced word down to its basic parts and give a suitable definition for each part. Ignore suffixes not covered in lessons.

1. Bryan is a real **"TECHNOPHILE"**; he loves the latest electronic gadgets.

2. Because of their light weight **DEHYDRATED** foods are ideal for campers.

3. **PSYCHOANALYSIS** is useful in treating a variety of mental disorders.

4. **ANADROMOUS** fish travel upstream from the sea to breed in fresh water.

5. Scientists doubt that life is possible on Venus's **ANHYDROUS** surface.

6. **ACYCLIC** compounds have string-like rather than ring-shaped molecules.

7. On July 4th the city's skies are filled with **PYROTECHNICAL** displays.

8. Your paper should contain a **BIBLIOGRAPHY** listing all your sources.

9. Student teachers must master both the science and art of **PEDAGOGY**.

10. Construction workers guard against **HYPOTHERMIA** during the winter.

MATCHING: Match the correct definition to the words listed below.

_____ acrolect   A. philosophy aiming to increase human knowledge

_____ anhydrosis   B. movement of an organism in response to light

_____ anthroposophism   C. deficiency or absence of perspiration in a person

_____ apyretic   D. free from fever or inflammation

_____ heliotaxis   E. delusion where one imagines to be a divine being

_____ hypogeal   F. standard language; most respected speech variety

_____ pedant   G. early symptom of disease; first attack of illness

_____ prodrome   H. government of scientists and similar experts

_____ technocracy   I. buried or located underground; subterranean

_____ theomania   J. a person excessively concerned with learning

BRIEFLY DEFINED: Give a short definition for the words listed below. Consult your dictionary for items you are unsure of.

Bible belt_____

cyclical _____

hypertension_____

pyrotechnics_____

sophomoric_____

discoveries

1. What is the difference between a hypercritical and a hypocritical person?

2. In previous lessons you encountered the <u>syn</u>- and <u>thes</u> root forms which combine to produce "synthesis" and "synthesize." What is the difference between "synthesis" and "analysis"? How do the root parts of these words account for this meaning difference?

3. Be careful to not confuse Greek <u>ped</u>, meaning 'child, training/instruction,' and Latin <u>ped</u>, meaning 'foot, move, progress.' Which of the following <u>ped</u> words come from the Greek and from the Latin <u>ped</u> root: pedant, pedate, pedestrian, pediatrics, pedigree, pedogenesis, pedometer, pedomorph?

4. A popular tourist attraction in Atlanta, Georgia, is the Cyclorama, where people can view a Civil War battle taking place all around them. Look up "cyclorama" in your dictionary for its meaning.

5. What and where is the Acropolis? What do the constituent parts of this word mean? Consult your dictionary for the following <u>acro</u>- words: acrocephaly, acromegaly, acronym, acropathy, acrophobia.

6. Tenth-graders and second-year college students are "sophomores." What is this word's curious etymology? What is "sophomoric behavior"?

7. Despite their similar appearances, "hypnosis," "hypnotic," and "hypnotize" do not come from the <u>hyp(o)</u> root. What is the etymology of these words?

8. The Church of England is the official church of the United Kingdom. Does that make Britain a theocracy? Why or why not?

9. What is the meaning of the following -<u>lysis</u> words: autolysis, cryptanalysis, electrolysis, hematolysis, hydrolysis, osteolysis, thermolysis?

10. Define the term "syndrome." Consult your dictionary for the following: China syndrome, Chinese restaurant syndrome, Stockholm syndrome.

11. Who were the Sophists? What is the difference between sophistry and sophistication?

12. What do the following acronyms stand for: AIDS, HIV, NOW, ROTC, SIDS, WASP. Explain how "radar" and "scuba" are also acronyms.

awakenings

The following words are formed from word roots introduced in this lesson and in previous ones. Consult your dictionary for words you are unsure of. Use this list to awaken your word sense and help you master this lesson.

acromegaly	demagogue	pedagogue
anagoge	dromedary	pedantic
analyze	encyclopedia	pedology
anhydrous	heliocentric	periderm
anticyclonic	heliozoic	psychoanalysis
antipyrine	hemolytic	pyrolysis
aphelion	hydrogenous	pyrometer
autolysis	hydrolysis	recycle
bibliographer	hydroponic	rehydrate
bibliolatry	hydrotactic	syndrome
bibliophile	hyperemia	theism
bicycle	hyper extend	theocracy
biotechnical	hyperthermia	theological
cyclical	hypodermic	theosophy
dehydrate	lysis	tritheism

27 roots

Root Form	Root Meaning	Examples
1. **agon**	struggle	prot**agon**ist
2. **alg**	pain	nost**alg**ia
3. **(a)esth**	feeling, perception	an**esth**esia
4. **gastr(o)**	stomach/belly, food	**gastro**nomy
5. **glot(t), gloss**	tongue, language	poly**glot**, **gloss**ary
7. **necro**	dead/death	**necro**philia
8. **nerv, neur**	nerve, nervous system	**nerv**ous, **neur**otic
9. **odont**	tooth	**odont**ology
6. **ortho-**	straight, correct	**ortho**doxy
10. **par(a)-**	beside, against, beyond	**para**llel
11. **phag**	feed/eat, swallow	eso**phag**us
12. **phras, phas, phat**	speak/say	**phras**e, a**phas**ia, em**phat**ic
13. **pne(u), pneum**	breath/breathe, lung	**pneum**onia
14. **thanas, thanat**	dead/death	eu**thanas**ia, **thanat**ology
15. **tox(ic)**	poison, harmful	anti**tox**in

notes

exercises

WORD ANALYSIS: Break each boldfaced word down to its basic parts and give a suitable definition for each part. Ignore suffixes not covered in lessons.

1. Josh's frequent attacks of **CARDIALGIA** were a big concern to his wife.

2. Alf is completing an adult education program in **PARALEGAL** studies.

3. A **PNEUMOGRAPH** can measure chest movements during respiration.

4. Muscles that counteract actions of other muscles are **ANTAGONISTS**.

5. **EUTHANASIA**, or "mercy killing," is a hotly debated topic these days.

6. A **PERIODONTIST** treats patients for gingivitis and other gum diseases.

7. **GLOTTOCHRONOLOGISTS** are experts in the history of languages.

8. **NEURALGIA** patients often experience sharp pains in joints and limbs.

9. A **PARADOX** is an apparent contradiction of facts that may also be true.

10. Hy suffered from painful **GASTRITIS** and needed constant medication.

MATCHING: Match the correct definition to the words listed below.

_____ aesthete   A. snail, slug, or similar crawling creature

_____ agon   B. contradiction/disagreement with established belief

_____ dysphagia   C. fortune-telling, clairvoyance, and the like

_____ dyspnea   D. inability or difficulty to swallow or take in food

_____ gastropod   E. specialist in treating teeth of young people

_____ gloss   F. conflict or dispute between characters in a drama

_____ heterodoxy   G. lover of beauty, especially in art or nature

_____ parapsychology H. blood poisoning

_____ pedodontist   I. shortness of breath; respiratory problem

_____ toxemia   J. brief explanation/translation of a technical word

BRIEFLY DEFINED: Give a short definition for the words listed below. Consult your dictionary for items you are unsure of.

anesthetic _____

esthetic _____

euthanasia _____

gastritis_____ _____

toxicology _____

discoveries

1. In certain charismatic Christian churches, members of the congregation are moved to glossolalia. What does this word mean? What is its etymology? If you have a Bible handy, turn to Acts 2:4 in the New Testament for mention of this phenomenon.

2. What does it mean to paraphrase a passage or text? What is a periphrastic construction in English?

3. Distinguish parameter from perimeter.

4. In Lesson 5 you were introduced to the Latin root para (meaning 'put in order, shield), which bears no relation to the Greek prefix para-. Which of the following words contain the Latin or the Greek para forms: parabola, parachute, parallel, paranoid, parapet, paraplegic, parasite, parasol?

5. When we are away from home and family, we might suffer from nostalgia. Consult your dictionary for this word's interesting etymology.

6. What is the meaning of these words ending in the - algia root: arthralgia, coxalgia, metralgia, myalgia, neuralgia, odontalgia, otalgia?

7. What is Orthodox Judaism? Relate the etymology of "orthodox" to its meaning when it is used to denote this branch of the Jewish faith.

8. Ortho- is a very productive prefix in English, appearing in dozens of words. Consult your dictionary for the meanings of these words, many of which you may not know: orthochromatic, orthoepy, orthogenesis, orthogonal, orthography, orthopteran, orthoscopic, orthostatic, orthotics.

9. What does the field of orthopedic medicine deal with? Relate the somewhat curious etymology of this word to its meaning.

10. Look up the word "pneuma." Relate its meaning to the pneu root. How is this word similar to "inspiration" and the Latin spir root?

11. One of the best known works by the 19th-century American poet William Cullen Bryant is "Thanatopsis." What is the theme of this poem?

12. What is a "detox" center of a hospital? What medical conditions would be treated in such a facility?

awakenings

The following words are formed from word roots introduced in this lesson and in previous ones. Consult your dictionary for words you are unsure of. Use this list to awaken your word sense and help you master this lesson.

antagonism	glossograph	paragraph
anthropophagy	macrophage	paralegal
aponeurosis	necrobiosis	paralysis
autotoxin	necrophile	parameter
cephalalgia	necrotomy	pedodontics
dysphagia	neuralgia	perineurial
emphasis	neuritis	periodontist
endodontia	neurobiology	periphrasis
endotoxin	neuron	phraseogram
esthete	neuropathy	pneumatolysis
euthanasia	neurotic	pneumograph
gastronome	odontoid	protagonist
gastroscope	orthodox	synesthesia
gastrotomy	orthopedics	telesthetic
glossary	orthoscope	toxoid

roots

Root Form	Root Meaning	Examples
1. -gon	angle/angled	octo**gon**
2. hect(o)-	hundred, many	**hecto**gram
3. hedr	side/face	deca**hedr**on
4. hemi-	half	**hemi**sphere
5. hept-	seven	**hept**achord
6. hex-	six	**hex**ameter
7. hol(o)	whole/entire	**Holo**caust
8. iso-	equal, same	**iso**dymanic
9. kilo-	thousand	**kilo**gram
10. mon(o)-	one, single	**mono**cle
11. pan(t)-	all, public/common	**pan**tomime
12. penta-	five	**Penta**teuch
13. poly-	many	**poly**gamy
14. prot(o)-	first/earliest, foremost	**proto**zoa
15. tetra-	four	**tetra**syllable

Note: The other Greek numbers have forms identical or very similar to their Latin counterparts. Refer to Lesson 16 for these forms.

notes

exercises

WORD ANALYSIS: Break each boldfaced word down to its basic parts and give a suitable definition for each part. Ignore suffixes not covered in lessons.

1. My father is known **POLYONYMOUSLY** as Robert, Bob, Rob, and Bert.

2. The **PENTAGON** is one of the most famous office buildings in the world.

3. In a number of Third World nations hunger and poverty are **PANDEMIC**.

4. Most Americans are **MONOLINGUAL;** they can speak only English.

5. The modern marathon is 26.2 miles or about 42.3 **KILOMETERS** long.

6. **HOLOGRAPHY** is a method for producing 3-dimensional images on film.

7. Rome's **PANTHEON**, built in 27 B.C., is a circular-shaped sacred temple.

8. An **ISOGLOSS** is a geographic boundary line for a dialect or an accent.

9. France is sometimes called "the **HEXAGON**" due to its geographic shape.

10. **MONOCHROME** monitors for computers are actually black and white.

MATCHING: Match the correct definition to the words listed below.

_____ dihedral   A. political system giving equal power to all citizens

_____ hectoliter   B. a solid geometric figure having 24 sides

_____ hemialgia   C. describing the shape of some pyramids

_____ hexapod   D. formed by or having two plane faces; two-sided

_____ isocracy   E. recognizing many gods but worshiping only one

_____ monolatry   F. an organism belonging to the insect class

_____ pentahedral   G. highly decorative or brightly colored work of art

_____ polychrome   H. primitive in structure or development

_____ protomorphic   I. pain affecting the right or the left side of the body

_____ trisoctahedron   J. unit of measure containing a little over 25 gallons

BRIEFLY DEFINED: Give a short definition for the words listed below. Consult your dictionary for items you are unsure of.

hectare_____

holistic_____

kiloton_____

Pan-American_____

protocol_____

discoveries

1. Words ending in the -gon suffix denote geometric figures. Arrange the following -gon words according to the number of angles/sides that each has: decagon, dodecagon, heptagon, hexagon, nonagon, octagon, pentagon, tetragon, trigon.

2. Consult your dictionary for the following words: Pentateuch, Heptateuch, Hexateuch. What is the meaning of the teuch root?

3. Look up "Jehovah"' and try to trace it to the word "Tetragrammaton." Connect this word to its etymology and to one of the Ten Commandments.

4. What is the connection between the hedr root meaning 'side/face' and the word "cathedral"? (This question may take some creative thinking on your part.) What does the phrase "ex cathedra" mean?

5. Contrast the meaning of words ending in the -gon and -hedron suffixes. Distinguish, for example, polygon/polyhedron and hexagon/hexahedron. Which of these would be studied in a plane geometry class? which in a solid geometry class?

6. The Greek root "myriad" often means 'countless.' It can be both a noun or an adjective, giving us phrases like "a myriad of political causes" and "myriad political causes." What is the specific number value of "myriad"?

7. One of the most horrific events in human history was the Holocaust. What was the Holocaust? How do its root parts contribute to its meaning?

8. A curious word in English is "triskaidekaphobia." What is its meaning?

9. What does the musical term "quaver" mean? What is a semiquaver? a demisemiquaver? a hemidemisemiquaver?

10. Define these poetry terms: dimeter, hexameter, pentameter, tetrameter, trimeter. What do the terms "dactylic," "iambic," and "trochaic" refer to?

11. The proto- prefix is often coupled with whole English words rather than with root parts. Define the following: protocontinent, protohistory, protohuman, protolanguage, proto martyr, prototype.

12. Consult your dictionary for the interesting etymology of pandemonium.

awakenings

The following words are formed from word roots introduced in this lesson and in previous ones. Consult your dictionary for words you are unsure of. Use this list to awaken your word sense and help you master this lesson.

bicephalous	kilocycle	pantograph
bipod	kilogram	pentagram
hectogram	monocephali	pentameter
hemimorphic	monochrome	polycentric
heptameter	monocycle	polygraph
hexagonal	monogram	polygyny
hexameter	monograph	polyphony
holandric	monohydrate	polysomic
hologram	monomania	protoderm
holography	monoglot	proton
isochronous	monophonic	protopathic
isocline	monopod	Tetragrammaton
isometric	panchromatic	tetrapod
isomorphic	pangram	trimeter
isostasy	panoptic	tripod

roots

Root Form	_Root Meaning_	_Examples_
1. all(o)-	other, different	**all**ergy
2. cat(a)-	down, against, back, very/completely	**cata**strophe
3. -clas(t)	break/destroy, broken	icono**clast**ic
4. dactyl	finger/toe/digit	**dactyl**ology
5. ethn	race/culture/people	**ethn**icity
6. ger(ont)	old/aged	**geront**ology
7. hagi(o)-	sacred, related to saints	**hagio**graphy
8. icon	image/likeness, idol	**icon**ic
9. kine, cine(ma)	move, motion picture	**kine**tic, **cinema**tic
10. met(a)-, meth-	beyond, after, changed, along with	**meta**phor, **meth**od
11. mnem, mne(s)	memory	**mnem**onic, **amnes**ia
12. paleo(nt)-	ancient/very old	**paleont**ology
13. pter	wing	helico**pter**
14. trop	turn, change	en**trop**y
15. troph	feed/nourish, grow	dys**troph**y

notes

exercises

WORD ANALYSIS: Break each boldfaced word down to its basic parts and give a suitable definition for each part. Ignore suffixes not covered in lessons.

1. The **PTERODACTYL** is an extinct flying reptile from the Jurassic period.

2. **ETHNOGRAPHY** deals with the scientific description of human culture.

3. If our muscles do not get enough exercise, they are subject to **ATROPHY**.

4. The city sometimes grants **AMNESTY** to people who owe parking fines.

5. **METALINGUISTICS** is the study of languages in their cultural contexts.

6. As part of their training physical therapists must study **KINESIOLOGY**.

7. **CINEMATOGRAPHY** is the art and technique of movie photography.

8. **ETHNOCENTRIC** people think their culture is better than other cultures.

9. An **APTERAL** temple has columns lining the front but none on the sides.

10. **PALEONTOLOGISTS** conduct their research on animal and plant fossils.

MATCHING: Match the correct definition to the words listed below.

_____ allonym   A. relating to mirrors and reflected images

_____ apotropaic   B. movement or growth of a plant in response to light

_____ apteryx   C. having extra fingers or toes

_____ catoptric   D. Greek goddess of memory; mother of the Muses

_____ Hagiographa   E. alias or assumed name taken by an author

_____ heliotropism   F. cell layer in the womb that feeds the embryo

_____ hyperdactylia   G. intended or designed to ward off evil spirits

_____ iconoscope   H. kiwi; other similar flightless bird

_____ Mnemosyne   I. early form of television-camera equipment

_____ trophoderm   J. in Judaism, a division of the Old Testament

BRIEFLY DEFINED: Give a short definition for the words listed below. Consult your dictionary for items you are unsure of.

catalysis_____

dystrophy_____

geriatrics_____

metaphoric_____

tropical_____

discoveries

1. A frequent meaning of the <u>trop</u> root is 'turn.' Connect this meaning to "tropic," "tropical," and other words denoting the area around the Earth's equator? Where are the Tropic of Cancer and the Tropic of Capricorn?

2. An infrequent use of the <u>trop</u> root comes in the literary term "trope" and in French-influenced "troubadour." Define these two words. What meaning does the <u>trop</u> root contain here?

3. Michael Jackson and Michael Jordan are icons of popular culture. What is a pop icon? What meaning does "icon" carry in computer technology?

4. Magicians are masters of telekinesis, which they accomplish through sleight of hand. What is telekinesis? Do you believe it is fact or fiction?

5. The <u>cat(a)</u>- prefix can be problematical, because its meaning is so variable, depending on roots it is appended to. Give the appropriate meaning of <u>cat(a)</u>- in the following words: cataclysm, catalepsy, catalog, cataplexy, catarrh, catatonic, catechism, cathode.

6. All universities are catholic, but only a few are Catholic. Explain.

7. The physically debilitating, usually fatal condition popularly known as ALS or Lou Gehrig's disease contains a root introduced in this lesson. Which one? What does ALS stand for?

8. A feature shared by many cartoon characters is tetradactylism. What does this mean? Identify a few of your favorite tetradactylous cartoon heroes.

9. The <u>dactyl</u> root appears in many biology-related words, including artiodactyl, brachydactylous, pamprodactylous, perissodactyl, zygodactyl. Define these terms.

10. Hypermnesia can accompany certain mental illnesses. What does this term mean?

11. What is the difference between "ethnic" and "ethic." What does the <u>eth</u> root which makes up "ethic" mean?

12. What is the difference between geriatrics and pediatrics? What is bariatrics? What is physiatrics?

awakenings

The following words are formed from word roots introduced in this lesson and in previous ones. Consult your dictionary for words you are unsure of. Use this list to awaken your word sense and help you master this lesson.

allograph	geotropic	metamorphosis
allonym	geriatrics	metasomatism
allopathic	gerontology	metastatic
anticatalyst	hagiographer	metonymy
archaeopteryx	Hagiographa	paleoanthropic
catarrh	hagioscope	paleobiochemistry
catastasis	heterotroph	paleography
catoptric	hierarchical	paleontology
cinematography	icon	psychokinesis
cinephile	iconoclast	psychotropic
dactylogram	iconographer	pterodactyl
dystrophic	iconolatry	syndactyl
ethnocentric	macropterous	synkinesis
ethnographer	metacenter	telekinesis
eutrophy	metalinguistic	tropotaxis

30   roots

Root Form	*Root Meaning*	*Examples*
1. **crypt**	hide/hidden, secret	en**crypt**ion
2. **dendr**	tree, bush	rhodo**dendr**on
3. **dyn(am)**	force/power	**dynam**ic
4. **gam**	marriage, sexual union	bi**gam**ist
5. **lit(h)**	stone	paleo**lith**ic
6. **naus, naut, nav**	ship, sail/sailor, (sea)sickness	**naus**eating, **naut**ical, **nav**y
7. **osteo**	bone	**osteo**pathy
8. **phor**	carry/bear	eu**phor**ia
9. **phot, phos**	light	**phot**ograph, **phos**phorous
10. **plas(t)**	form, shape	proto**plas**m
11. **poli**	city, govern/control	metro**poli**tan
12. **pseud(o)-**	false	**pseudo**scientific
13. **spher**	ball/globe	bathy**spher**e
14. **top**	place, local, field	**top**ical
15. **xeno-**	stranger, foreign	**xeno**phobic

notes

exercises

WORD ANALYSIS: Break each boldfaced word down to its basic parts and give a suitable definition for each part. Ignore suffixes not covered in lessons.

1. Bats and similar **PHOTOPHOBIC** creatures will venture out only at night.

2. **HIERAPOLIS** in present-day Turkey was an early center of Christianity.

3. Genealogical tables are **DENDRIFORM** diagrams that show our "roots."

4. With its many cultures and cuisines, London is very **COSMOPOLITAN**.

5. North, Central, and South America make up the Western **HEMISPHERE.**

6. Prehistoric cultures often erected huge **MEGALITHS** as monuments.

7. Jay complains **AD NAUSEAM** about work; he should stop complaining.

8. **CRYPTOCLASTIC** materials are made of microscopic rock fragments.

9. **BIODYNAMIC** farming uses organic fertilizers rather than chemicals.

10. **PHOSPHORUS** is an essential ingredient in matches and many fireworks.

MATCHING: Match the correct definition to the words listed below.

_____ agamic   A. abnormal development of tissues and cells

_____ autogamy   B. configured in an irregular or deceptive manner

_____ dendrite   C. foolish; not wise or prudent

_____ dysplasia   D. in literary study, a traditional theme or motif

_____ impolitic   E. reproducing without male/female cells; asexual

_____ lithosphere   F. process whereby plants fertilize themselves

_____ monolithic   G. mineral that bears a branching form or outline

_____ pseudomorphic   H. said of offspring that differ markedly from parents

_____ topos   I. uniform or unvarying in constitution or makeup

_____ xenogenetic   J. the earth's rocky or solid crust

BRIEFLY DEFINED: Give a short definition for the words listed below. Consult your dictionary for items you are unsure of.

cryptanalysis _____

lithograph _____

misogamist _____

photosynthesis _____

xenophobe _____

discoveries

1. The philodendron is a popular house plant. Its etymology (<u>phil</u> + <u>dendr</u>) suggests that it is a 'lover of trees.' Consult the etymological information of "philodendron" for the explanation of this.

2. A popular shrub that one sees in this country is the rhododendron. What does this bushy plant look like? What does the <u>rhodo</u> root mean?

3. Most of us are familiar with the term "bigamy," which means the practice of having two spouses at the same time. A very similar word is "polygamy," which meaning having two <u>or</u> <u>more</u> spouses. What does "digamy" mean? In this country bigamy and polygamy are illegal. Is digamy legal or illegal?

4. Distinguish a metaphor from a simile? How/why are both metaphoric?

5. According to some grammarians, the phrase "I feel nauseous" is incorrect. Look up "nauseous" and "nauseated" in your dictionary. Does it make a distinction between these two words? Explain how "I feel nauseous" could be considered an incorrect usage.

6. What is topiary art? What is a topical ointment used for?

7. Look up the word "utopia." What is its etymology? Who wrote the famous essay *Utopia* in 1535? In what way was this author's life far from utopian?

8. Consult your dictionary for the following: Bigfoot or Sasquatch, Yeti or the abominable snowman, the Loch Ness Monster. Why might they be of interest to cryptozoologists?

9. In what ways do the following periods of the Stone Age trace technological advancements by humans: Eolithic, Paleolithic, Mesolithic, Neolithic?

10. Osteoclasis requires orthopedic surgeons "to break in order to repair." Explain.

11. A number of famous authors have written under a pseudonym. What does this word mean. Give an example or two of pseudonymous authors.

12. From this and previous lessons, you are already familiar with the <u>astr</u>, <u>hydr</u>, <u>phot</u>, and <u>therm</u> roots. Without using a dictionary, define these <u>dynam</u> words: astrodynamic, hydrodynamic, photodynamic, thermodynamic.

awakenings

The following words are formed from word roots introduced in this lesson. Consult your dictionary for words you are unsure of. Use this list to awaken your word sense and help you master this lesson.

allogamy	dynamometer	osteoid
Apocrypha	dyne	osteolysis
apocryphal	dysphoric	osteopathic
aquanaut	dystopia	osteoplasty
astronautical	ecosphere	phosphorescent
biosphere	endogamy	photophobic
chromatophore	euphoria	plasma
chromo lithography	exogamy	plasticity
cosmonaut	geopolitical	polygamy
cosmopolitan	gonophore	spherical
crypt	hyperplastic	spherometer
cryptogram	nauseous	telephotography
dendriform	nautilus	topical
dendrology	naval	xenolith
dynamo	osteogenesis	xenophobia

index of latin roots

Below are all prefixes, roots, and suffixes that make up the "Roots" lists on the first page of each Latin lesson. Other word parts that appear only in the "Discoveries" exercises are not listed. The number in parentheses denotes the lesson number.

A

ab-, a-, abs-: away **(6)**

acu, acr, acer(b), acid: sharp, point **(17)**

ad-, a-, ac-, af-, ag-, al-, am-, an-, ap-, ar-, as-, at-: to/toward, cause/make **(3)**

ag, ig, act: do/act **(6)**

alt, al, ol, ul: high, grow/grown, feed/support **(17)**

ama, amor, am, em, im, m: love, friendly **(10)**

amb(i), am: around, on both sides **(5)**

ambl, ambul: walk, move/go **(8)**

anim: life/live, mind, soul/spirit **(5)**

ann, en(n): year **(15)**

ante, anti: before, old **(4)**

apt, ept: fit, capable **(17)**

aqu: water **(20)**

art, ert, arm: skill, capability, weapon **(17)**

aud, audit: hear, listen **(3)**

aug, augur, auct, aux: increase, divine, help **(12)**

aur: ear, hear **(3)**

B

ben-, bon, bount: good/well, generous **(1)**

bi-, bin-, bis-, du: two **(16)**

C

cal, calor: heat **(19)**

cand, cens, cend, cin(d), ciner: fire/burn, white, glow/shine, ashes **(19)**

cap, capt, ceipt, ceiv, cept, cip, cup: take, contain, begin **(4)**

cap, capit, chap: head, principal, property/money **(2)**

carn: meat, flesh **(17)**

ced, ceed, cess: move/go, withdraw, yield/let go **(7)**

cent: hundred, hundredth **(16)**

cern, cert, cre, cret, crit: decide, separate **(7)**

cid, cad, cas, cis: cut, kill/die, fall, event/accident **(7)**

circum, circ: around **(4)**

cli, clin, cliv: lean/tend toward, bed, support **(20)**

clud, clus, claus, clo(s), clois, clav: close/shut/lock, lock, settle, alone **(20)**

con-, co-, col-, com-, cor-: together/with, very, cause **(2)**

contr, counter: against **(2)**

cord: nice/agree, heart, remember **(3)**

corp, corpor: body **(3)**

cred, cre: believe, trust **(1)**

cresc, creas, cre, cru: grow/growth **(12)**

crim, crimin: judge, accuse, crime **(7)**

cruc, cru: cross, torment, important test **(12)**

cub, cumb: lie, hollow **(14)**

cumber, cumbr: hinder/hindrance **(8)**

cult, col: dwell, till, worship **(11)**

cur, sur: care, attention **(8)**

cur, curr, curs, corr, cours: run, hasty, path **(8)**

D

de-: down, away, very **(3)**

dec-: ten, tenth **(16)**

dent: tooth, hole/pit **(3)**

dia, di: day **(15)**

dict, dica: speak, order, set forth/proclaim **(1)**

dis-, di-, dif-: not, apart/away, opposite **(2)**

div, de(i): god, foretell **(11)**

doc, doctr: teach accept **(9)**

dom, domin: house, control, master/lord **(11)**

don, dat, dit, dos, dot, dow: give **(17)**

dorm: sleep/rest **(14)**

duc, duct: lead **(2)**

dur: lasting, hard **(15)**

E

equ: fair, even/same, value **(5)**

err: wrong, wander/go **(7)**

-esce: becoming, growing **(17)**

ev: age **(15)**

ex-, e-, ef-: out of, former **(2)**

extr, exter: outside, beyond **(8)**

F

fa, fam, fess: speak, spoken of, rumor **(12)**

fac, fect, fic, fi, -fy: make/do/deed **(1)**

fam(il): household, know **(10)**

feder: league/union **(10)**

fer: carry, bear/birth **(3)**

fid: faith **(1)**

fig, fict, fing, fix, -fy: shape/make, invent, fasten **(12)**

fil(i): child/offspring, related **(10)**

fin: end, border, pay/pay off **(13)**

flam, flagr: burn, blaze, bright **(19)**

flect, flex: bend **(5)**

flor, flour, foli, foil: flower, plant/growth, leaf, sheet **(20)**

flu(v), fluct, flux: flow **(18)**

frag, fract, frang, fring: break, piece **(5)**

frater, fratr: brother, allied **(10)**

fus, fund, found: pour, melt/blend **(18)**

G

gen, gend, gener, gn: race, kind, produce, origin/inborn **(1)**

gest, ger: carry, offer, clog **(12)**

grad, gred, gress: step/unit, go/move **(9)**

grand: great, full-grown **(4)**

greg: flock/group **(11)**

H

hab(it), habil, hibit, ab(i)l, ib(i)l: have/hold, dwell, capable, suitable for **(17)**

hes, her: stick/cling **(13)**

hom, homin, hum: human, earth, low **(10)**

I

in-, il-, im-, ir-, em-, en-: in, not, cause, very **(1)**

inter-, intel-: between/among **(6)**

intra-, intro-: within **(6)**

J

ject, jac, jet: throw, send, situated **(9)**

jun(c)t, join, jug: connect/join, impose **(13)**

jur, judic, judg, just: oath, right, judge **(7)**

L

lat, later: side, wide, support **(20)**

lat: carry/bear, bring **(20)**

lav, lu(v), lut, lug: wash, pour **(18)**

leg, legis, lect: law, charge/appoint, read, bequeath/grant **(6)**

leg, lig, lect: choose/gather, esteem/care for **(6)**

lig, li(a), ly, loy: bind, connect **(20)**

limit, limin: threshold **(13)**

ling, langu: language, tongue **(6)**

linqu, lic: leave/forsake, permit **(12)**

liter: letter/writing **(6)**

loc, locat: place **(4)**

locu, loqu: speak **(4)**

lud, lus: play, deceive **(19)**

lum(en), lumin, luc, lust(e)r: light, clear, easily seen **(19)**

M

magn, maj, max: large **(4)**

mal-: bad/badly **(1)**

man(u), main: hand, do **(2)**

mand, mend: order, require, praise **(2)**

mat(e)r, metr: mother, womb/origin, substance **(10)**

medi: middle, near **(15)**

mem(or): recall **(13)**

ment, mon, min, men, mount: think, advise, warn/threaten, serve, project/mountain, lead **(13)**

migr: move/travel **(8)**

mill: thousand, thousandth **(16)**

mis, mit, miss, mess: send, allow **(5)**

mis-: wrong **(5)**

misc, mix: mix **(20)**

mod, med, mens: style, measure, take measures **(14)**

moll: soft **(20)**

mor(t): dead/death **(19)**

mov, mob, mot: move, drive **(8)**

multi: many **(11)**

N

nat, gnat, nasc, gnit: source, born, tribe **(10)**

nec, noc, nox, nuis: harm **(19)**

nihil, nil, nul(l): nothing **(14)**

noc(t), nox: night **(15)**

non(a), nov(em): nine, ninth **(16)**

non-, ne-, neg-, neu-: not, deny **(14)**

numer: number **(14)**

O

ob-, o-, oc-, of-, op-: against, bad, not, very/to **(8)**

oct-: eight, eighth **(16)**

omni: all **(11)**

ora, or: formal speech, pray **(12)**

P

par, per: beget, produce **(20)**

par(t), peer, pair, port: equal/same, part, share **(5)**

par, para, pair: put in order, shield **(5)**

parl, par, parol: discourse, promise **(6)**

pater, patr: father, support, homeland **(10)**

pau, pauc, pov: few/little **(14)**

pecc: sin, fault **(7)**

pecu: wealth, one's own **(17)**

ped: foot, move, progress **(2)**

pend, pens: pay, give **(14)**

pend, pens, pond: consider, hang **(14)**

per-, pel-: through, each, very, bad **(8)**

sub-, suc-, suf-, sup-, sur-, sus-: under, after, less than, small/minor **(9)**

sult, sa(i)l, sil, sau(l)t: jump/leap, attack **(19)**

super-, sur-, supr-, sum(m): over, more than, large/major, total, highest **(9)**

T

tac, tic: silent **(6)**

tang, tact, tag, tig, ting: touch, rely/depend **(4)**

temp, temper, tempor: time, state/condition, moderation **(15)**

tempt, tent: attract, try, touch **(13)**

ten, tin, tent, tain: hold, keep **(13)**

tend, tens, tent, tenu: stretch, lean toward, heed, thin/delicate **(13)**

ter(r): earth, ground **(20)**

tort, tors, tor: twist/turn, crooked **(8)**

tot: all, whole **(14)**

tract, tra, trai, treat: draw/drag, treat/care **(13)**

trans-, tra-: across/beyond, through **(3)**

tri-, ter(t)-: three, third **(16)**

U

ultra-, ult: final, beyond, other **(9)**

un(i)-: one **(16)**

V

vac, va(i)n, void: empty, leave, vain, shun **(18)**

val, vail: good/well, farewell, strong, useful **(19)**

ven, vent: come **(3)**

ver: true/truth **(2)**

verb: word **(6)**

verg: bend, incline toward **(5)**

vert, vers, vort: turn, highest point **(4)**

vid, vis, voy: see **(2)**

vir, virtu: man, true/real, skill **(10)**

vit, viv: life/live **(1)**

voc, vok: voice, call **(3)**

vol: wish/will **(6)**

volv, volu: roll/turn, arise from **(5)**

vor: eat **(17)**

vulg: common, low **(11)**

vuls: pull, shake **(20)**

index of greek roots

Below are all prefixes, roots, and suffixes that make up the "Roots" lists on the first page of each Greek lesson. Other word parts that appear only in the "Discoveries" exercises are not listed. The number in parentheses denotes the lesson number.

A

a-, an-: not without **(21)**
ac(m)-, acro-: top/summit, sharp, extremity/tip **(26)**
agog: teach/instruct, induce **(26)**
agon: struggle **(27)**
alg: pain **(27)**
all(o)-: other, different **(29)**
ana-: back/again, up/upon **(22)**
and(e)r: man, maleness **(21)**
ant(i)-: against **(22)**
anthrop: human **(21)**
ap(o)-: back, again, up/upon **(25)**
arch, archa(e): rule, first, foremost **(23)**
ast(e)r: star, heavens **(23)**
aut(o)-, taut(o)-: self, same **(22)**

B

bi(o): life **(21)**
bibl(io): book **(26)**

C

cac(o)-: bad/badly **(23)**
card: heart **(24)**
cat(a)-: down, against, back, very/completely **(29)**
cent(e)r: center **(21)**
cephal: head **(24)**
chem: substance, chemical **(24)**
chir: hand **(24)**
chrom(at): color **(22)**
chron: time **(22)**
-clas(t): break/destroy, broken **(29)**
cosm: universe/world, order **(23)**
-crat, -cracy: rule/govern **(22)**

crypt: hide/hidden, secret **(30)**
cycl: circle, wheel **(26)**

D

dactyl: finger/toe/digit **(29)**
dem: people **(22)**
dendr: tree, bush **(30)**
derm(at): skin **(24)**
dia-: through, across **(22)**
dox: belief **(25)**
drom: run, course **(26)**
dyn(am): force/power **(30)**
dys-: bad/badly, difficult **(25)**

E

ec-, ect(o)-, ex(o)-: out of/outside **(23)**
eco: household, environment **(23)**
ectom: surgical removal **(25)**
en(do)-, em-: in **(21)**
encephal: brain **(24)**
ep(i)-: upon, over, after, also **(24)**
erg, urg: work **(25)**
(a)esth: feeling, perception **(26)**
ethn: race/culture/people **(29)**
eu-: good, genuine **(23)**

G

gam: marriage, sexual union **(30)**
gastr(o): stomach/belly, food **(27)**
ge(o): earth **(21)**
ger(ont): old/aged **(29)**
glot(t), gloss: tongue, language **(27)**
-gon: angle/angled **(28)**
gram, graph: write, record **(21)**

gyn(ec): woman, femaleness **(21)**

H

hagi(o)-: sacred, related to saints **(29)**
hect(o)-: hundred, many **(28)**
hedr: side/face **(28)**
heli(o): sun **(26)**
hem(at), em: blood **(24)**
hemi-: half **(28)**
hept-: seven **(28)**
hetero-: different **(25)**
hex-: six **(28)**
hier(o): holy/sacred **(23)**
hol(o): whole/entire **(28)**
hom(e)o-: same/alike **(25)**
hydr: water, liquid **(26)**
hyp(o)-: under/below, partial **(26)**
hyper-: over/above, more than **(26)**

I

iatr: medical treatment **(24)**
icon: image/likeness, idol **(29)**
iso-: equal, same **(28)**
-itis: inflammation **(24)**

K

kilo-: thousand **(28)**
kine, cine(ma): move, motion picture **(26)**

L

-lat(e)r: worship **(23)**
lit(h): stone **(30)**
log: idea, word, speech, reason, study **(21)**
lys, lyt, -lyz: break down, loosen **(26)**

M

macro-: large **(25)**
manc, mant: prophesy **(23)**
mani(a): madness, mad desire **(22)**
mega(lo)-: great/very large **(25)**
met(a)-, meth-: beyond, after, changed, along with **(29)**
met(e)r: measure **(23)**
mnem, mne(s): memory
micro: small **(25)**
mis(o): hate **(21)**
mon(o)-: one, single **(28)**
morph: shape/form **(23)**

N

naus, naut, nav: ship, sail/sailor, (sea)sickness **(30)**
ne(o): new **(22)**
necro: dead/death **(27)**
nerv, neur: nerve, nervous system **(27)**
nom: system, law **(23)**

O

odont: tooth **(27)**
-oid: resembling/like **(21)**
onym, onom(at): name **(22)**
ops, opt: eye, sight, examine **(25)**
ortho-: straight, correct **(27)**
osteo: bone **(30)**

P

pale(o)-: ancient/very old **(29)**
pan(t)-: all, public/common **(28)**
par(a)-: beside, against, beyond **(27)**
path: disease, feel **(21)**
ped: child, training/education **(26)**
penta-: five **(28)**
peri-: around **(23)**
phag: feed/eat, swallow **(27)**